Bread Machine Cookbook

D1609535

Quick-Easy and Delicious Recipes for Beginners

ROXANNE WHITEHEAD

Contents

Introduction

Would you want to know how to always have freshly made bread on your kitchen table without having to spend several hours kneading and baking in your kitchen?

If you answered "yes," continue reading...

Bread machines may be a great addition to any kitchen counter, but few people understand how to utilize them to their full potential, limiting themselves to a few standard bread recipes and praying for the best.

A bread machine is a basic but flexible kitchen gadget that can help you quickly create a variety of tasty bread at home.

You'll be able to enjoy fragrant, fresh, and mouth-wateringly wonderful handmade bread every day since baking bread in a bread maker takes so little time and is so handy.

However, anytime we attempt new things, there is a chance that we may fail.

Even when making bread in a bread machine, baking is a science, and there are several ways for an experiment to go wrong.

You may have made a batch of dough that won't rise, or your bread is excessively dry, collapsed, or shaped like a mushroom.

But don't be alarmed by this.

Learn all there is to know about bread machines, so you don't make the same errors.

This handbook will walk you through every step of the process, and you'll uncover a plethora of mouthwateringly delicious bread recipes that will have your family begging for more.

The following are some of the things you'll learn in this book:

- Easy Bread Machine Recipes: You can prepare right in your own home.

- There is no longer any space for error: Learn about the most frequent bread-making challenges and how to prevent them for a consistently successful batch of bread.

- Know how to use your bread machine: Learn all the capabilities of your bread maker and make the most of it. There will be no more messing with all the buttons.

- Beginner-friendly: The Absolute Beginners Loaf is a great place to start. A foolproof recipe that will take you through the whole process of making your handmade bread.

- To convert your favorite recipes, follow these steps: Keep your family tradition alive by using this instruction to make your mother's recipes in your bread machine. There is no such thing as an ancient or difficult recipe.

- Ideal for folks who are always on the go: With just half the work, you may enjoy delicious loaves of bread right away. In no time, these loaves will be devoured.

Chapter 1: The Bread Machine

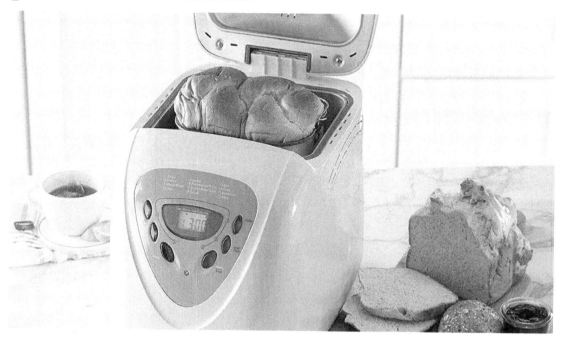

1.1 Pros and Cons

Making our bread at home has become a family custom for decades, and despite advances in baking equipment, people still like making bread at home. The enthusiasm for baking is growing, from simple sandwich bread recipes to elaborate specialty loaves. Bakers, like bread, come in a variety of shapes and sizes. Some of us make bread often, while others do it just sometimes. Some of us bake for a single person or two, while others bake for huge crowds. Regardless, one could wonder whether purchasing a bread maker is the best option for them. Is it true that bread makers save time and labor at the expense of taste? Is it true that homemade bread has a higher quality? Your grandma may believe it, but it doesn't mean it's true. Let's continue reading to discover out.

Pros of Using a Bread Machine:

1.) Bread Machines Save Time.

While you must adhere to a recipe, it usually entails merely placing items in a machine and allowing it to handle the rest. The machine does the kneading, proofing, and baking of the bread for you. This enables you to concentrate on other chores while you wait, saving you a lot of time if you have a busy schedule.

2.) Bread Machines Are Simple to Use.

The dishes are typically simple and require little to no talent on the cook's part. This is excellent news for folks who are new to baking. Once you've gotten the hang of things, you may branch out and attempt something a little more creative by reading some bread machine recipe books. Soon, you'll be able to mix your favorite bread recipes with your favorite dishes for a delectable palate-pleasing combo.

3.) Bread Machines Are Consistent.

Bread makers relieve a lot of the pressure that comes with baking. There isn't much space for mistakes, and the outcomes are always consistent. This means that if you discover a recipe you like, you can stick to it and receive the same result every time you bake, much like purchasing a loaf from your favorite brand at the store. Comfort food like that is invaluable, and it will quickly pay for your bread maker.

Cons of Using A Bread Machine:

1.) Bread Machines Are Expensive.

Like any other home equipment, buying a cheap bread machine is never smart since they are unstable and have limited lifespans. It's certainly worth the additional money to invest in a genuine machine that's well made and lasts a long time, and there are many high-quality bread makers to select from. Of course, the next concern is whether you'll utilize the computer sufficiently to justify the investment. Probably not if you just bake once or twice a month. If you bake a couple of times a week, investing in a bread machine is a fantastic idea.

2.) Bread Machine Loaves Aren't as Tasty.

While bread machines are time-saving and efficient, they also create bread that lacks the distinctive flavor of freshly baked bread. Handmade bread is often denser, while machine bread is fluffier and airier. Handmade has a thicker, chewier crust and is more fragrant and savorier. The flavor/scent of machine bread is a little blander, and the crust is thinner and crispier. Those who aren't choosy about their bread, especially children, won't notice the alterations. This makes the bread machine ideal for families who want to produce bread for packed lunches and quick meals throughout the week. It's ideal for preparing bread by hand and baking it in the oven if you're making it as a genuinely authentic and tasty side dish for a gourmet dinner.

3.) Bread Machines Are Restrictive

While they may make several recipes, bread machines are very restricted in what they can make. Handmade is by far the finest option for various forms, sizes, tastes, and styles. The only change between each loaf is the form and size, with the ingredients being the only variance. This may detract from the enjoyment of making your bread and pushes the bar closer to homemade being the preferable option.

1.2 Bread Machine Cycle Stages

When you push the start button, what happens?

Cycles are the many processes that your bread machine goes through.

These bread machine cycles are, for the most part, the same across the board.

Kneading

The kneading cycle is the first and, by far, the most crucial stage in preparing yeast bread. Kneading thoroughly incorporates all the ingredients and is likely your bread machine's noisiest cycle. This cycle might take anywhere between 15 and 45 minutes. The amount of time it takes depends on your bread maker and the sort of bread you're making. There are usually kneading paddles at the bottom of the baking pan that fully mix everything.

Rest Cycle

The rest cycle allows the dough to rest before it resumes kneading. This is known in the baking world as autolyzing the dough. In other words, it permits the gluten and starch in the dough to absorb all of the moisture in the air. This cycle might take anything from a few minutes to over 35 minutes.

Rise Cycle

If your bread contains gluten, it will need this cycle to rise or lift properly. This is what gives bread its fluffy, airy texture. This includes increasing the dough's temperature slightly and allowing the years to ferment. This cycle will take roughly 40-50 minutes, depending on your bread machine. It might sometimes take a long time, particularly if you're making French bread.

Punch Cycle

The Punch Cycle begins once your dough has finished the rise cycle. The punching cycle gets its name because your bread machine starts kneading the dough all over again during this cycle. The difference is that it's done much more softly at this step to release the small gas bubbles created by yeast fermentation during the rise cycle. Punch, also known as the form cycle, is a quick cycle that takes just a few seconds to complete, but it's still vital.

Bake

Finally, we've arrived at my favorite cycle. The baking processes. This is when your bread maker starts baking your bread. Depending on your bread maker and the sort of bread you're baking, this cycle might take anywhere from 30 mins to over 90 minutes.

Different Bread Machine Cycles and Cycle Times

Depending on the kind of bread you're baking, your bread maker will employ a mix of various cycles. Some bread will need more than one rising cycle or kneading cycle. Some do, while others do not. It all depends on the sort of bread you're making and the bread maker you're using. We'll show you how the cycles appear for some of the most often used parameters in the sections below.

Basic Bread

Your go-to cycle will most likely be the Basic White Bread cycle. You'll want to utilize it the bulk of the time. It's also a flexible cycle that can create anything from white bread to potato bread to garlic bread. This cycle, which usually takes 3 to 4 hours to complete, runs like this.

Sweet Bread

This cycle is for baking bread with sweet ingredients such as dried fruit, nuts, and powdery additions like sugar or cinnamon. Because of these components, your bread will cook considerably quicker, requiring the bread machine to cook it at a lower temperature. If you bake sweet bread using this cycle, your bread will be delicious; your bread will be burned

if you use any other cycle. The standard sweet bread cycle on a bread maker is shown below. The baking time is around 3 hours.

The following is a typical bread machine cycle for making sweet bread:

Rise – Punch – Second Rise – Shape – Final Rise – Bake Knead – Rest – Second Knead

The only difference between the cycle and the bake cycle is the bread machine's temperature.

Whole-Wheat Cycle

Whole wheat or the whole grain bread cycle is generally included in bread machines and is used to make loaves that include a lot of whole wheat or cracked grain. This cycle is used to make doughs with a lot of gluten. This dough takes extra rising and kneading time to be cooked correctly.

Rise – Punch – Second Rise – Shape – Final Rise – Bake – Knead

French Bread

Another popular bread machine cycle is French. This bread is special because it has a thicker crust than basic bread, requiring more time for the three primary cycles of kneading, rising, and baking.

Rise – Punch – Second Rise – Shape – Final Rise Knead – Rest – Second Knead

A loaf of French bread will normally take four hours from start to finish.

Gluten-Free Bread

You don't have to give up bread just because you're gluten-free. You can create gluten-free bread anytime you want using your bread machine's gluten-free cycle. Because there is no gluten to mix around in the bread, the Gluten-free option bakes bread quicker than the other settings. As a result, kneading takes significantly less time, and baking takes less time. Kneading, rising, and baking This cycle may usually be completed in under two hours.

Rapid Bake

You won't find a speedy cycle in every bread machine, but if yours does, like the Oster Express bake, you're in for a treat. This cycle can bake basic white bread in under 90 mins, and if it's a smaller loaf, it can be done in less than an hour with the Oster Express Bake.

Kneading, rising, and baking

Cake And Jam

Did you know that your bread machine can bake cakes and even make jam? Yes, this can be used for more than simply baking bread; it can also be used to make marmalade, jams, and even sweets like cakes.

Typical Jam Cycle

Mix time – 10 mins

Cook time– 45 mins

Typical Cake Cycle

Mix time– 20 mins

Cook time– 60 mins

Chapter 2: Beginner's Guide

2.1 How to Store Your Bread?

Bread boxes aplenty, paper above plastic, freeze over the fridge. Madelyn Osten, head baker of Sullivan Street Bakery's Miami location, shares the most important steps for keeping bread properly, so you can get the most out of your favorite loaf while preventing mold, crust, and moisture.

In 2017, the New York-based company, started in 1994 by James Beard Prize baker Jim Lahey, carried its highly praised bread south. Sullivan Street, a manufacturing plant in Miami's Little Haiti district, bakes and distributes rustic bread to various restaurants, country clubs, hotels, and other locations around the South Florida region. They've also just formed a retail collaboration with Milam's Market, which makes bread storage even more critical to their business.

Freeze your bread

"The best approach to keep that crusty loaf for as long as possible is to freeze it." Wrap firmly, whole or cut, in a freezer bag. When we freeze slices, we prefer to place wax paper between them to simplify pulling out just what we need. The best approach to defrost a completely frozen loaf is to leave it in the fridge overnight; it may become soggy on the counter, and although it will toast alright, it will be a nicer loaf in the fridge. When defrosting, don't forget to unwrap from the freezer bag. While it defrosts, this prevents any water from accumulating. Don't worry if defrosting sounds daunting: you can always reheat bread directly from the freezer. Try baking an entire loaf at 325°F for 25–30 minutes, while pieces may be toasted immediately in the toaster."

A fresh loaf of bread should be consumed within two to three days after purchase. If you're going to eat it straight away, storing it in a paper bag on the table is the way to go. While preserving bread in plastic may seem a good idea, it increases mold development, causing the bread to spoil much more quickly. We also keep our bread heels and use them to cover the cut side of my loaf. Maintaining the freshness of your loaf by keeping the cut side as exposed as possible is also a good idea." Bread boxes are your buddies " Bread boxes are a wonderful way to add beauty to your kitchen while also keeping bread fresh. They contain tiny holes, allowing a little air to flow and preventing the bread from molding. Toss in a piece of bread with your loaf if you're worried about pests and prefer to store bread in an airtight container. The slice with the most surface area will draw water and aid in moisture management in your container."

It's crucial to know where you'll keep your bread.

It's just as essential to keep your bread as how you keep it. Isn't it true that bread belongs on top of the refrigerator? Please try again. Refrigerating bread causes paper-bagged bread to dry and plastic-bagged bread to mold quickly. This is due to the excessive heat produced by your refrigerator. The same goes for keeping bread near a dishwasher; the additional heat and moisture. This equipment emits is not good for bread. Bread should be kept in a cool, dry place in your kitchen. If not on the counter, tuck it away in a cupboard or a deep drawer."

Get some reusable bread bags.

"Try a reusable bread bag if you're searching for a more adaptable or environmentally responsible method to store your bread. There are many more on the market these days, and many of them are machine washable and freeze well. Take them to the supermarket with you and drop in that new bread straight away. These may be a good substitute for a paper bag, which is prone to tearing and always seems to let crumbs fall onto the counter. Reusable bags are composed of permeable fabrics and function similarly to paper bags, but without the trash. They're a terrific investment for a bread (or environment) lover of any degree, ranging from $7 to $20."

2.2 Tips for Bread Machine

1. Place the ingredients in the machine in the correct sequence. You start with the liquids and then go on to the dry components in most machines. The yeast is the final component to be added. We create a little depression in the mound of flour for the yeast. This prevents it from coming into touch with the liquids until the machine begins working.

2. Understand your machine's flour capacity. This is required to pick a correctly scaled recipe. One approach to figuring this out is to consult your machine's manual (or check it up online) to see what it says about its capacity in pounds.

4.) Most machines will be 1 pound, 1.5 pound, or 2-pound machines. A 1-pound machine will handle around 2 cups of flour, a 1.5-pound machine about 3 cups, as well as a 2-pound machine about 4 cups if you don't have that information. If you're unsure, start with a recipe that calls for no more than 3 cups of flour and gradually increase as you gain expertise.

3. Open the cover around 5 or 10 minutes into the dough-making cycle, and if the machine is straining (loud clunking sounds) or the dough seems dry, add a tablespoon of water at a time. A lovely, compact dough ball should be seen.

4. If the dough seems gloopy or soupy, add extra flour – gently – until a beautiful ball is formed. The top will shrink while baking if the dough is too loose, and although it will taste OK, it will not be particularly attractive.

5. Don't get too worked up if you just have a simple machine with a few cycles (sweet, French, whole wheat etc.).

6. If you're managing your fat consumption, replace the butter or oil in the recipe with applesauce. If you don't have any, butter powder may be used instead of oils or stick items. You will, without a doubt, be rewarded with exceptional flavor.

7. Make sure you use genuine sugar. Sugar feeds the yeast and aids in the rising of the dough. Honey or molasses may be substituted, but sugar substitutes must be avoided. They are not going to work.

8. You may reduce the amount of salt in the recipe by half. It doesn't seem to make a difference in the end outcomes.

9. All-purpose flour is not the same as bread flour. It contains more protein and gluten, and it is required for your bread to have a fine grain.

10. If the bread rises beautifully but falls flat when baked, it either rises too quickly or the recipe is too big. Next time, reduce the amount of yeast or sugar used or pick a recipe that uses less flour overall.

11. Some loaves are thick and weighty by their very nature. This is particularly true if you use a large percentage of whole grains. If this occurs with white loaves, consider reducing the salt, which prevents the bread from rising.

12. If you're not happy with the results of your whole-wheat loaves, try this approach. Allow the machine to complete its kneading process. Then restart the machine after turning it off. This will lead to a longer kneading time, which might be the key to success with whole wheat and grain bread.

13. Whether you're having trouble, ask yourself if the flour is fresh. It will be alright if you use flour that has been kept appropriately (cold, dark, low humidity - sound familiar?). But if it's been sitting in a 90-degree garage for the previous five years, well, you get the picture. In the cupboard, we keep my daily flour in a huge bucket. This is not an issue for me since my residence is rather cool. We keep flour in my freezer and Mylar bags with oxygen absorbers for longer-term preservation.

14. Although we like to produce artisan bread and pizzas using the "artisan bread in five" technique, you may also take the dough from the mixer after the kneading cycle and shape it into a loaf, rolls, or pizza to bake in a regular oven or even in your Dutch oven.

2.3 Common Bread Making Issues

Your yeast is inactive.

Maybe your yeast has spent too much time in your kitchen. Alternatively, you might have destroyed the yeast by mixing it with too hot water – the recommended temperature for water in most bread recipes is approximately 105-110 F: warm but not hot. In either case, the yeast isn't effectively activated to perform its function. Check the expiry date on your yeast and make sure your water or liquid temperature matches the temperature mentioned in the recipe for optimal results.

Your kitchen is too cold.

If your kitchen resembles a refrigerator, this might be the cause of your dough's failure to rise. Bread rises best when kept at a somewhat warm room temperature. It might take substantially longer to rise at a lower temperature. Allow the dough to rise for an extended time or put it in a warmer location.

Your dough develops a "skin."

Your bread dough acquires a crusty surface or "skin" during the first rising or the proving process. This is mainly due to a lack of dough coverage. Because you don't want your bread to produce a crust before it bakes, most recipes ask for covering the dough throughout both rising times.

Your bread rises, then falls.

Consider the following scenario: Your bread is rising and baking wonderfully in the oven. Then, suddenly, it flattens out in the middle. If your loaf has a valley in the center, one of these factors is probably to blame:

Too much liquid.

The dough will not rise properly if it is overly moist. Reduce the liquid content by a tablespoon or two.

Too much yeast.

Make sure you read your recipe thoroughly. While most people purchase yeast in packets, not all recipes need the full package. The bread will rise quickly and collapse if you use too much yeast.

The wrong type of yeast.

Similarly, using the incorrect yeast might change the outcome of a dish. If you use rapid-rise yeast in a recipe that calls for normal yeast, the result may be an unfavorable rising and falling effect.

Not enough salt.

Did you use less salt than the recipe asked for (or forget to use any at all)? This may be to fault. Because salt inhibits yeast's rise, missing it may have the same effect as adding too much yeast: a quick rise followed by a large deflation. If you believe you may have measured improperly in the future, just attempt the recipe again. If you're certain you followed the instructions to the letter, try one of these remedies (not all at once) and see if it works.

Your bread is too dry.

Even if your bread was only taken out of the oven a few hours ago, it seems to be dry. Here are a few possible reasons and solutions:

You used whole grains.

If you use whole-grain flour in place of part or all the flour in the recipe, your bread may become dry. To compensate for the "thirstier" and more absorbent grains, you need to add a bit of extra liquid to the recipe while preparing whole-grain bread. More tips for making whole grain bread may be found on this page.

Not enough protein.

Can you tell me what kind of flour you used for baking your bread? Bread flour has a greater protein content, which helps your bread stay moist. If you believed you could replace the higher protein flour in your recipe with cake flour, it might be fault for the dry texture.

Your bread is still gooey inside.

Your bread seems great on the outside, but the inside is still doughy when cut. This is usually due to one of two factors:

You didn't bake the bread long enough.

How can you tell when the bread is done? Check the interior temperature of most bread: 190 F indicates that it is thoroughly cooked within.

The oven wasn't hot enough.

Although if you set your oven to the temperature specified in the recipe, this does not guarantee that the temperature was reached. Ovens come in a variety of shapes and sizes. Make sure yours is correct by putting a thermometer inside.

Your bread is burnt on top.

Your bread is nicely cooked, but the top has turned black. This doesn't necessarily imply that you did anything incorrectly; it just signifies that the top browned too quickly.

If the top of the bread seems to be browning too soon the next time, avoid the feared burned top by tenting the top with foil, like a pie crust, to protect the top from browning too quickly.

Your bread has hard white bits inside.

This one is simple: you didn't knead the dough sufficiently, and parts of flour formed clumps that didn't mix in. Sift the flour first to make sure it's lump-free, then knead the dough well to eliminate any lumps before letting it rise.

Too many holes.

It's fine to have a few holes, but what about enormous empty pockets? Not at all. Are your bread inside more like Swiss cheese than a sandwich vessel? Most likely, you neglected to deflate or punch the dough. This little step is critical for achieving a solid "crumb" in your bread.

Your bread enlarges strangely through baking.

If your bread becomes out of the oven with odd growths all over it, it's probably because you failed to score it. Although not all loaves need scoring on the top, many do. This generates little "vents" that allow heat to escape and even expand the bread. The bread might grow in surprising ways if it isn't scored.

Overly condensed bread.

There are a few possibilities for why your bread feels like a stone. Here are a few examples:

Inadequate rising or proofing time.

It's tempting to skip the extended rising times and get the dough into the oven as soon as possible. However, if you don't give your bread enough time to rise, it may wind up being flatter and heavier than you'd prefer.

Inactive yeast.

You may have unwittingly stopped the bread dough from rising correctly if you killed the yeast with too-hot water or used stale yeast. A thick loaf of bread might arise because of this. Make careful to verify your yeast's expiry date and use lukewarm (105-110 F) water or liquid in your recipe.

Incorrect protein content in your flour.

If you use flour with low protein content, the dough will not rise as much as it should. Super-high protein flours, such as whole-grain flours, might, however, make your bread heavier. When creating the dish in issue, be sure you use the right flour. You'll discover additional tactics and strategies as you practice making bread, which will help you produce excellent loaves every time.

2.4 Bread Machine Troubleshoot Guide

1. Small and Heavy Loaf

Check your measures and double-check the flour-to-liquid ratio, which should be between 212 and 3 cups flour to 112 cups liquid.

Check to see whether the yeast is still OK and hasn't expired.

During the kneading stage, check the dough's consistency. You may need to add extra liquid or flour.

2. Gummy Texture

Here are some suggestions to prevent your bread from being underbaked.

To ensure that heat reaches the middle of the bread, make sure the pan is big enough for the recipe.

Make sure your bread maker is set on the correct setting. A light crust setting, for example, may not be long enough to bake certain rich bread recipes fully. If you have the choice, choose a darker setting.

3. Collapsed Loaf

It's never joyed to open your bread machine to see a collapsed or sunken loaf. Here are a few things you can do to ensure it doesn't happen again.

Make sure the pan you're using is big enough for the recipe.

Make sure your dimensions are correct (be ensure the ratio of flour to liquid is exact).

During the kneading stage, check the dough's consistency.

Use no more yeast than the recipe calls for.

Be careful to add the salt as specified in the recipe, since it is necessary for the structure of the bread.

4. Mushroom-Shaped Loaf

Make sure the pan you're using is big enough for the recipe.

Make sure you measure your ingredients correctly and according to the recipe's instructions.

During the kneading round, check for uniformity.

If the weather in your location is hot, check the final tip under Collapsed Loaf.

5. Open, Holey Texture

Make sure your dimensions are correct (be sure the ratio of flour to liquid is exact).

During the kneading round, check for uniformity.

Use no more yeast than the recipe calls for.

As stated in the recipe, season it with salt.

If the weather in your location is hot, check the final tip under Collapsed Loaf.

6. Bumpy, Uneven Top/Very Dense Texture

Check that you're using the right flour by softly spooning it into a dry measuring cup and leveling it off with a straight-edged utensil.

Make sure you don't use too much flour. You may also check the dough consistency while kneading to see if the extra liquid is needed.

Chapter 3: Bread Making & Baking Ingredients

Here's a list of the baking items you'll need to produce delicious homemade bread, muffins, banana bread, and more. Always keep these items in your pantry. This will enable you to rapidly prepare a variety of delicious handmade bread and sweet fast bread to serve your hungry family.

Whole Wheat Flour

These are a few important baking and bread-making ingredients to always have on hand.

Baking Soda

Baking soda and powder

Salt

White sugar, Brown sugar, confectionery sugar, and other sugars

Yeast - yeast for bread machines, active dry yeast, quick yeast, and so forth.

Basic Pantry Items

Leavening Agents (i.e., Yeast & Baking Powder) – You should use FRESH leavening agents for all of your recipes. If you use old/stale ingredients (yeast or baking soda), your bread and banana may not rise.

Baking Powder - We aim to use baking powder free of aluminum in our recipes.

Baking Soda - Don't use the baking soda that has been deodorizing your refrigerator for the previous two years while preparing banana bread or cookies. It's possible that you won't obtain the best outcomes.

Active Dry Yeast — For oven-baked bread, this yeast is often used. It's not yeast from a bread maker.

Bread Machine Yeast - One of the most important bread machine components is new/active bread machine yeast. For bread baking, dead yeast is not a good thing.

Sourdough Yeast - This yeast will assist you in making delectable sourdough bread.

Bread Machine Yeast

Butter

Vegan Butter Unsalted Butter Tip – Vegetable oil may frequently be used to substitute butter in many recipes (if you run out of butter and can't get to the grocer).

Chocolate & Related Ingredients – Our M&M chocolate chip, chocolate chip banana bread muffins, and white chocolate chip cookies are just a few of our favorite chocolate-based dishes. Updated

Baking Cocoa - Baking cocoa is often used to give cakes and cookies a "chocolaty" color and taste.

Butterscotch Chips — Butterscotch chips are a must-have ingredient in recipes like butterscotch banana bread and butterscotch chocolate chip cookies.

Chips with Caramel

Chocolate Chunks are larger chocolate chunks.

Chips of Dark Chocolate

Chips of Milk Chocolate

Mini Chocolate Chips — These are the smaller chocolate chips we used to decorate our chocolate chip banana muffins.

Semi-Sweet Chocolate Chips M&M's

Chips of White Chocolate

Eggs – Organic eggs may be purchased at your local store. It's possible that eggs aren't the ideal candidates for a company's free delivery policy.

Flour & Related Ingredients – Flour is one of the most important baking components. Always keep extra flour in your cupboard.

All-Purpose Flour is often used in cakes, cookies, and other baked goods.

Almond Flour Bran — Adding fiber and roughage to your bread is simple with almond flour bran.

Bread Flour - When preparing bread, bread flour is typically the best flour to use.

Cake Mix with Buckwheat Flour – This enables you to prepare cakes and our world-famous cake mix banana bread.

Cornmeal made with coconut flour - You can't create tasty, sweet cornbread muffins without cornmeal.

Gluten-Free Flour — Gluten-free flour is used in our delicious gluten-free chocolate chip banana bread.

Multigrain Cereal - This cereal is used in the production of multigrain bread.

Potato Flour (Organic Flour)

Rice flour is flour made from rice.

Rye Flour - This flour is ideal for baking rye bread sandwiches.

Self-Rising Flour — This kind of flour already has baking powder in it.

Whole Wheat Flour - Get some whole wheat fiber in your diet by eating whole wheat flour.

Fruit (Dried) – Many recipes call for dried fruit, such as golden raisin banana bread, cranberry bread, and chocolate chip cranberry cookies.

Apples

Apricots

Chips made from bananas

Blueberries

Cherries

Cranberries

Strawberries

Dates

Raisins

Pears

Figs

Raisins, Golden

Mangoes \oranges

Pineapples

Prunes

Milk & Related Ingredients

Instant Milk —powder of Instant milk is an excellent backup if you come to an end of milk in the fridge in the middle of a recipe.

Organic Milk made from oats

Milk made from soy

Mixes – You can purchase a pre-made baking mix if you don't wish to purchase big quantities of ingredients for a particular meal (and therefore won't have a lot of leftover ingredients).

Mixes for Banana Bread

Biscuit Preparations

Mixes for bread

Mixes for Beer Bread

Bread Mixes with Cheese

Mixes for cornbread

Soda Bread Mixes from Ireland

Mixes for Whole Wheat Bread

Mixes for Brownies

Mixes for cakes

Cookie dough mixes

Muffin Preparations

Mixes for Quick Bread

Nuts & Related Ingredients

Almond Butter Almonds

Cashew Butter Cashews

Hazelnuts

Nutella Peanuts with Hazelnut Butter

Pecans with Peanut Butter

Sunflower Butter Pecan Butter

Walnuts

Butter made with walnuts

Oats & Oatmeal

Oatmeal, Old Fashioned — This adds huge oat "flakes" to bread and other dishes. Oat flakes are used in oatmeal bread, banana bread, and other baked goods.

Organic Oats One Minute Oatmeal

Oil (Vegetable)

Canola Oil

Olive Oil

Corn Oil

Vegetable Oil

Quick Bread Ingredients – These ingredients may create pumpkin bread, applesauce bread, and other baked goods.

Applesauce Pumpkin Puree — You'll need this to prepare the machine pumpkin bread, stove pumpkin cranberry bread, and other baked goods.

Salt

Sea salt

Himalayan pink salt

Kosher salt

Spices

Black pepper

Allspice

We produce our chives in our garden for a genuinely natural and organic component. Of course, dried chives are an option if you take it easy.

Garlic Powder with Cinnamon

Ginger - There can't be any gingerbread if there isn't any ginger.

Italian Seasonings — For Italian Herb Bread, this is a must-have spice. It's made up of herbs, including oregano, sage, rosemary, and thyme.

Onion Powder with Nutmeg

Oregano

If you want to add a little zing to your bread, use red pepper flakes.

Rosemary is a flavorful herb that may make rosemary bread or Italian-style bread.

Vanilla Extract - Vanilla extract is often used in cooking (like banana bread and cookies).

pepper (white)

Sugar & Related Ingredients

White granulated sugar

Molasses

Sugar cane

Brown sugar

Turbinado sugar

Other Essential Baking Ingredients

Cheese

Mozzarella cheese

Pepper jack cheese

Cheddar cheese

Potato flakes

Chapter 4: White Bread Recipes

4.1 Buttermilk Bread II

Prep time: 20 mins

Cook time: 35 mins

Servings: 24

Ingredients

- Buttermilk 1 ½ cups

- Warm water ½ cup (110 degrees F/45 degrees C)

- Margarine ½ cup

- White sugar ¼ cup

- Baking soda ½ teaspoon

- Active dry yeast 2 (.25 ounce) packages

- Salt 2 teaspoons

- Bread flour 5 ½ cups

Instructions

1. Warm water is used to proof yeast.

2. In a small saucepan, combine the butter or margarine and the buttermilk. Slowly heat until the butter or margarine has completely melted. Allow cooling to be lukewarm.

3. Combine the sugar, buttermilk mixture, salt, baking soda, and yeast in a large mixing bowl. Using the dough hook part of an electric mixer, add 3 cups of flour one at a time. Continue to mix while gradually adding the remaining flour. Turn the dough onto a lightly floured surface until it is no longer sticky. Knead the dough for several mins, or until it is soft & smooth. Turn once in an oiled mixing bowl. Allow the dough to rise until it has doubled in size.

4. Punch the dough down. Divide the dough into two loaves. Place in two 8 x 4-inch bread pans that have been properly oiled. Allow dough to rise until it is one inch higher than the pans.

5. Preheat the oven to 375 degrees F (190 degrees C) and bake for 30 to 35 minutes. When knocked, the loaves should be pleasantly golden and hollow sounding.

Nutritional values

Calories: 49 kcal | Proteins: 0.8 g | Fats: 3.9 g | Carbs: 3.1 g

4.2 White Bread

Prep time: 5 mins

Cook time: 3 hrs.

Servings: 12

Ingredients

- Warm water 1 cup (110 degrees F/45 degrees C)

- White sugar 3 tablespoons

- Salt 1 ½ teaspoons

- Vegetable oil 3 tablespoons

- Bread flour 3 cups

- Active dry yeast 2 ¼ teaspoons

Instructions

1. Combine the water, sugar, oil, salt, bread flour, and yeast in the bread machine's pan.

2. Preheat oven to 350°F and bake on the White Bread setting. Before slicing, cool on wire racks.

Nutritional values

Calories: 168 kcal | Proteins: 4.4 g | Fats: 4 g | Carbs: 28.3 g

4.3 Best Bread Machine Bread

Prep time: 10 mins

Cook time: 40 mins

Servings: 12

Ingredients

- Warm water 1 cup (110 degrees F/45 degrees C)
- White sugar 2 tablespoons
- Bread machine yeast 1 (.25 ounce) package
- Vegetable oil ¼ cup
- Bread flour 3 cups
- Salt 1 teaspoon

Instructions

1. Combine the water, sugar, and yeast in the bread machine's pan in the water, sugar, and yeast. Allow 10 minutes for the yeast to dissolve.

2. Toss the yeast with the oil, flour, and salt. Press Start after selecting the Basic or White Bread option.

Nutritional values

Calories: 174 kcal | Proteins: 4.3 g | Fats: 5.2 g | Carbs: 27.1 g

4.4 Traditional White Bread

Prep time: 20 mins

Cook time: 30 mins

Servings: 20

Ingredients

- Active dry yeast 2 (.25 ounce) packages
- White sugar 3 tablespoons
- Warm water 2 ½ cups (110 degrees f/45 degrees c)
- Lard softened 3 tablespoons
- Salt 1 tablespoon
- Bread flour 6 ½ cups

Instructions

1. Dissolve yeast & sugar in warm water in a large mixing bowl. Combine the lard, salt, and two cups of flour in a mixing bowl. 1/2 cup at a time, add the remaining flour, mixing thoroughly after each addition. When the dough has come together, turn it onto a floured surface and knead for approximately 8 minutes, or until smooth and elastic.

2. Lightly grease a large mixing bowl, then set the dough in it and turn to coat it with oil. Cover with a moist towel and set aside in a warm place to rise for 1 hour or until doubled in volume.

3. Turn the dough floured surface to deflate it. Form the dough into two loaves by dividing it into two equal portions. Place the loaves in two 9x5-inch loaf pans that have been gently oiled. Cover the loaves with a moist towel and let rise for approximately 40 minutes, or until doubled in volume.

4. Preheat the oven to 425 degrees Fahrenheit (220 degrees C).

5. Place the bread in the oven and reduce the temperature to 375 degrees F. (190 degrees C). Bake for 30 minutes, or when the top is golden brown, and the bottom of the loaf sounds hollow when tapped.

Nutritional values

Calories: 167 kcal | Proteins: 4.9 g | Fats: 2.6 g | Carbs: 30.4 g

4.5 Asian Water Roux White Bread

Prep time: 20 mins

Cook time: 30 mins

Servings: 20

Ingredients

- Water ½ cup
- White sugar 1 tablespoon
- Butter ¼ cup
- All-purpose flour 1 cup
- Active dry yeast 2 ½ teaspoons
- Warm water ¾ cup
- All-purpose flour 3 cups
- White sugar ⅓ cup
- Instant dry 3 tablespoons milk powder
- Salt 1 teaspoon

- Egg 1
- Melted butter, 2 teaspoons divided

Instructions

1. To prepare the water roux, heat 1/2 cup water to a boil in a small saucepan, then whisk in 1 tablespoon sugar and the butter, combining to dissolve the sugar. 1 cup flour, 1 cup boiling liquid, 1 cup flour, 1 cup boiling liquid, 1 cup flour, 1 cup flour, 1 cup flour, 1 cup flour, 1 cup flour, 1 cup flour, 1 cup flour, 1 cup flour, 1 cup flour, 1 cup flour, 1 cup flour, 1 cup flour, 1 cup flour, 1 Refrigerate the bowl overnight, covered with plastic wrap.

2. Bring water roux to room temperature the following day. Stir the yeast with 3/4 cup warm water in the work bowl of an electric stand mixer and let it aside for 5 to 10 minutes, or until a creamy layer develops on the top. Combine 3 cups flour, 1/3 cup sugar, salt, dry milk powder, and an egg in a mixing bowl. Scoop the water roux into the mixing bowl with spoonfuls and knead the dough on low speed for approximately 2 minutes to properly integrate the ingredients. Increase the mixer speed to medium & knead for another 8 minutes, or until the dough is soft and smooth.

3. Turn the dough out into an oiled bowl, cover gently with a towel, and let rise for 1 hour in a warm location. Punch the dough down.

4. 2 8x4 inch loaf pans, greased

5. Cut the dough in half on a floured board and shape each half into a loaf shape. Put the dough in the preheated loaf pans, cover loosely with a towel, and let rise for another hour or until doubled in size.

6. Preheat the oven to 350 degrees Fahrenheit (175 degrees C). 30 to 40 minutes in a preheated oven, bake the loaves until the tops are softly golden brown. Remove it from the pans while the bread is still warm and brush it with melted butter.

Nutritional values

Calories: 139 kcal | Proteins: 3.5 g | Fats: 3.2 g | Carbs: 23.8 g

4.6 Chef John's White Bread

Prep time: 20 mins

Cook time: 30 mins

Servings: 10

Ingredients

- Whole milk, warmed 1 ¼ cups
- Active dry yeast 1 (.25 ounce) package
- Egg, beaten 1 large

- White sugar 1 tablespoon

- White vinegar 1 tablespoon

- Baking soda ¼ teaspoon

- Fine salt 1 teaspoon

- Cayenne pepper 1 pinch

- All-purpose flour, 2 ¾ cups or more as needed

- Unsalted butter, 3 tablespoons very soft

For the Top:

- All-purpose flour, 1 tablespoon or as needed

- Melted butter, 2 tablespoons divided

Instructions

1. Warm the milk in a stand mixer bowl equipped with the dough hook. Pour yeast on top and dissolve for 10 to 15 minutes, or until a few little bubbles appear. Combine the beaten egg, sugar, salt, cayenne pepper, vinegar, baking soda, flour, and butter in a mixing bowl.

2. Knead the dough at low speed until it starts to come together. Increase the pace a little and knead for another 3 minutes. Scrape the sides clean with a spatula and collect the dough into the middle. Cover and let rise for 1 1/2 to 2 hours, or until doubled volume.

3. Using butter, grease a spatula and a loaf pan. Using the spatula, scrape the dough into the pan. To equally spread the dough, smooth out the top. Dust the top with flour and gently push the dough to smooth it out. Allow 30 minutes for the dough to rise in the pan.

4. Preheat the oven to 350°F (180°C) (175 degrees C).

5. Cut a deep slice lengthwise across the middle of the bread using a sharp knife or razor. You may have to go over it multiple times. Most of the melted butter should be applied to the top.

6. Bake for 30 minutes in a preheated oven till golden brown.

7. Brush the remaining butter over the heated loaf. Allow 10 minutes for cooling in the pan before turning out onto a wire rack to cool for almost 1 hour before slicing.

Nutritional values

Calories: 211 kcal | Proteins: 5.6 g | Fats: 7.6 g | Carbs: 29.8 g

4.7 Amish White Bread

Prep time: 20 mins

Cook time: 40 mins

Servings: 24

Ingredients

- Warm water 2 cups (110 degrees F/45 degrees C)
- White sugar ⅔ cup
- Active dry yeast 1 ½ tablespoons
- Salt 1 ½ teaspoons
- Vegetable oil ¼ cup
- Bread flour 6 cups

Instructions

1. Dissolve the sugar in hot water in a large mixing bowl, then whisk in the yeast. Allow yeast to proof until it looks like a creamy foam.

2. In a mixing bowl, combine the yeast, salt, and oil. Mix in one cup of flour at a time. Knead the dough until it is smooth on a lightly floured board. Place dough in a well-oiled bowl and toss to coat. Using a moist towel, cover the dish. Allow 1 hour for the dough to double in size.

3. Knead the dough. Knead for a few mins before dividing into two halves. Form into loaves and put in two 9x5 inch loaf pans that have been thoroughly greased. Allow for a 30-minute rise time, or until the dough has risen 1 inch over the pans.

4. Preheat oven to 350°F (175°C) and bake for 30 minutes.

Nutritional values

Calories: 168 kcal | Proteins: 4.4 g | Fats: 2.9 g | Carbs: 30.7 g

4.8 Focaccia Bread

Prep time: 20 mins

Cook time: 15 mins

Servings: 12

Ingredients

- All-purpose flour 2 ¾ cups

- Salt 1 teaspoon

- White sugar 1 teaspoon

- Active dry yeast 1 tablespoon

- Garlic powder 1 teaspoon

- Dried oregano 1 teaspoon

- Dried thyme 1 teaspoon

- Dried basil ½ teaspoon

- Ground black pepper 1 pinch

- Vegetable oil 1 tablespoon

- Water 1 cup

- Olive oil 2 tablespoons

- Grated parmesan cheese 1 tablespoon

- Mozzarella 1 cup

Instructions

1. In a large mixing bowl, combine the flour, salt, garlic powder, sugar, yeast, oregano, thyme, basil, and black pepper. Combine the vegetable oil & water in a mixing bowl.

2. Turn the dough onto a lightly floured board and knead till smooth and elastic. Lightly oil a large mixing bowl then set the dough in it and turn it to coat it with oil. Cover with a moist towel and set aside for 20 minutes to rise in a warm location.

3. Preheat the oven to 450 degrees Fahrenheit (230 degrees C). Place dough on a buttered baking sheet after punching it down. Make a 1/2-inch-thick rectangle out of the dough. Apply a thin layer of olive oil on the top. Parmesan and mozzarella cheeses are sprinkled over the top.

4. Bake for 15 minutes, or till golden brown, in a preheated oven. Warm the dish before serving.

Nutritional values

Calories: 171 kcal | Proteins: 6 g | Fats: 5.8 g | Carbs: 23.4 g

4.9 Jo's Rosemary Bread

Prep time: 10 mins

Cook time: 40 mins

Servings: 12

Ingredients

- Water 1 cup

- Olive oil 3 tablespoons

- White sugar 1 ½ teaspoons

- Salt 1 ½ teaspoons

- Italian seasoning ¼ teaspoon

- Ground black pepper ¼ teaspoon

- Dried rosemary 1 tablespoon

- Bread flour 2 ½ cups

- Active dry yeast 1 ½ teaspoons

Instructions

1. Place the bread machine pan ingredients in the manufacturer's suggested sequence. Select the white bread cycle and click the Start button.

Nutritional values

Calories: 138 kcal | Proteins: 3.6 g | Fats: 3.9 g | Carbs: 21.6 g

---

4.10 Good 100% Whole Wheat Bread

Prep time: 5 mins

Cook time: 3 hrs.

Servings: 12

Ingredients

- Active dry yeast 1 ½ teaspoons
- Whole wheat flour 3 cups
- Salt 1 ½ teaspoons
- White sugar 1 ½ tablespoons
- Nonfat dry 1 ½ tablespoons milk powder
- Margarine 1 ½ tablespoons
- Warm water 1 ¼ cups (110 degrees f/45 degrees c)

Instructions

1. Place the bread machine pan ingredients in the manufacturer's suggested sequence.
2. Select between the Whole Wheat or the Basic Bread option. Start by pressing the Start button.

Nutritional values

Calories: 124 kcal | Proteins: 4.7 g | Fats: 1.9 g | Carbs: 24 g

---

4.11 Whole Wheat Honey Bread

Prep time: 5 mins

Cook time: 3 hrs.

Servings: 12

Ingredients

- Water 1 ⅛ cups

- Whole wheat flour 3 cups

- Salt 1 ½ teaspoons

- Honey ⅓ cup

- Dry milk powder 1 tablespoon

- Shortening 1 ½ tablespoon

- Active dry yeast 1 ½ teaspoons

Instructions

1. Place the bread machine pan ingredients in the manufacturer's suggested sequence. Select the Whole Wheat option, then push the Start button.

Nutritional values

Calories: 148 kcal | Proteins: 4.6 g | Fats: 2.2 g | Carbs: 30 g

4.12 Buttermilk Honey Wheat Bread

Prep time: 2 mins

Cook time: 3 hrs.

Servings: 12

Ingredients

- Active dry yeast 2 ½ teaspoons

- Whole wheat flour 1 cup

- All-purpose flour 2 cups

- Baking soda ½ teaspoon

- Salt 1 teaspoon

- Honey 3 tablespoons

- Vegetable oil 1 ½ tablespoons

- Buttermilk, 1 ½ cups at room temperature

Instructions

2. In a bread machine pan, combine the yeast, whole wheat flour, all-purpose flour, baking soda, oil, salt, honey, and buttermilk.

3. If using a bread machine, set the temperature to medium.

4. To knead dough in an oven, use the manual or dough cycle. Remove the bread from the machine and set it in a prepared loaf pan. Allow rising until it has doubled in size. Bake for 25 minutes in a 350°F (175°C) oven, or until the bottom of the loaf sounds hollow when tapped.

Nutritional values

Calories: 156 kcal | Proteins: 4.9 g | Fats: 2.4 g | Carbs: 29.3 g

4.13 Maple Whole Wheat Bread

Prep time: 5 mins

Cook time: 5 mins

Servings: 12

Ingredients

- Whole wheat flour 2 ½ cups

- Bread flour ½ cup

- Salt ⅓ teaspoon

- Water 1 ¼ cups

- Maple syrup 4 tablespoons

- Olive oil 2 tablespoons

- Active dry yeast 1 ½ teaspoons

Instructions

1. Put the ingredients in the bread machine saucepan in the manufacturer's suggested sequence. Select the wheat bread cycle and click the Start button.

Nutritional values

Calories: 144 kcal | Proteins: 4.3 g | Fats: 2.8 g | Carbs: 26.9 g

4.14 Honey Whole Wheat Bread

Prep time: 5 mins

Cook time: 3 hrs.

Servings: 10

Ingredients

- Warm water 1 ⅛ cups (110 degrees F/45 degrees C)

- Honey 3 tablespoons

- Salt ⅓ teaspoon

- Whole wheat flour 1 ½ cups

- Bread flour 1 ½ cups

- Vegetable oil 2 tablespoons

- Active dry yeast 1 ½ teaspoons

Instructions

1. Toss the ingredients into your bread machine according to the manufacturer's instructions. Use the light color setting and the wheat bread cycle.

Nutritional values

Calories: 180 kcal | Proteins: 5.2 g | Fats: 3.5 g | Carbs: 33.4 g

4.15 Almond Bread

Prep time: 10 mins

Cook time: 3 hrs.

Servings: 12

Ingredients

- Water 1 ¼ cups

- Almond oil 4 teaspoons

- Salt 1 teaspoon

- Honey ¼ cup

- Almond flour 1 cup

- Whole wheat flour 2 cups

- Vital wheat gluten ¼ cup

- Xanthan gum 1 teaspoon

- Dry yeast 1 (.25 ounce) package

Instructions

1. In a bread machine, combine water, honey, almond flour, almond oil, salt, whole wheat flour, xanthan

gum, essential wheat gluten, and yeast, in that order. For a 2-pound loaf, follow the manufacturer's directions.

Nutritional values

Calories: 117 kcal | Proteins: 4.6 g | Fats: 1.9 g | Carbs: 22 g

4.16 Flax and Sunflower Seed Bread

Prep time: 10 mins

Cook time: 30 mins

Servings: 15

Ingredients

- Water 1 ⅓ cups

- Butter softened 2 tablespoons

- Honey 3 tablespoons

- Bread flour 1 ½ cups

- Whole wheat 1 ⅓ cups bread flour

- Salt 1 teaspoon

- Active dry yeast 1 teaspoon

- Flax seeds ½ cup

- Sunflower seeds ½ cup

Instructions

1. In the bread machine pan, place all ingredients (excluding sunflower seeds) in the order indicated by the manufacturer.

2. Select the Basic White Cycle and click the Start button. When the Knead Cycle's signal sounds, add the sunflower seeds.

Nutritional values

Calories: 140 kcal | Proteins: 4.2 g | Fats: 4.2 g | Carbs: 22.7 g

4.17 Easy Whole Wheat Bread

Prep time: 10 mins

Cook time: 3 hrs.

Servings: 12

Ingredients

- Warm water ¾ cup (110 degrees F/45 degrees C)

- Powdered egg substitute 1 tablespoon (Optional)

- Vegetable oil 2 tablespoons

- Sugar 2 tablespoons

- Salt 1 teaspoon

- Whole wheat flour 1 cup

- Bread flour 1 cup

- Rapid rise yeast 1 teaspoon

Instructions

1. In a bowl of warm water, dissolve the egg replacement. Add all ingredients in the bread machine pan in the manufacturer's suggested sequence. Press Start after selecting Whole Wheat cycle & Regular bake time.

2. After 5 minutes, examine how the dough is kneading; it may need 1 tablespoon of flour and 1 tablespoon of water depending on the consistency. Allow the bread to cool completely on a wire rack before cutting.

Nutritional values

Calories: 65 kcal | Proteins: 1.7 g | Fats: 2.5 g | Carbs: 9.6 g

4.18 Steakhouse Wheat Bread

Prep time: 10 mins

Cook time: 3 hrs.

Servings: 8

Ingredients

- Warm water ¾ cup
- Butter softened 1 tablespoon
- Honey ¼ cup
- Salt ½ teaspoon
- Instant coffee granules 1 teaspoon
- Unsweetened cocoa powder 1 tablespoon
- White sugar 1 tablespoon
- Whole wheat flour 1 cup
- Bread flour 1 cup
- Bread machine yeast 1 ¼ teaspoons

Instructions

1. In the pan of a bread machine, add the warm water, coffee, cocoa, sugar, bread flour, butter, honey, salt, whole wheat flour, & bread machine yeast in the sequence stated. Set the machine on a normal or basic cycle with a light crust.

Nutritional values

Calories: 167 kcal | Proteins: 4.5 g | Fats: 2.1 g | Carbs: 34.2 g

4.19 High Protein Bread

Prep time: 10 mins

Cook time: 2 hrs. 30 mins

Servings: 10

Ingredients

- Active dry yeast 2 teaspoons
- Bread flour 1 cup

- Soy flour ¼ cup

- Powdered soy milk ¼ cup

- Whole wheat flour 1 cup

- Oat bran ¼ cup

- Canola oil 1 tablespoon

- Honey 1 tablespoon

- Salt 1 teaspoon

- Water 1 cup

Instructions

1. Put ingredients in the saucepan of the bread machine in the order suggested by the manufacturer. Choose basic medium or standard-setting; click Start.

Nutritional values

Calories: 137 kcal | Proteins: 6.5 g | Fats: 2.4 g | Carbs: 24.1 g

4.20 Seven Grain Bread II

Prep time: 10 mins

Cook time: 1 hr. 30 mins

Servings: 8

Ingredients

- Warm water 1 ⅓ cups (110 degrees F/45 degrees C)

- Active dry yeast 1 tablespoon

- Dry milk powder 3 tablespoons

- Vegetable oil 2 tablespoons

- Honey 2 tablespoons

- Salt 2 teaspoons

- Egg 1

- Whole wheat flour 1 cup

- Bread flour 2 ½ cups

- 7-grain cereal ¾ cup

Instructions

1. Place the ingredients in the bread machine saucepan in the manufacturer's suggested sequence.

2. Select the Whole Wheat Bread cycle and press the Start button.

Nutritional values

Calories: 285 kcal | Proteins: 9.8 g | Fats: 5.2 g | Carbs: 50.6 g

4.21 Ezekiel Bread

Prep time: 15 mins

Cook time: 40 mins

Servings: 10

Ingredients

- Milk ½ cup

- Water ½ cup

- Egg 1

- Olive oil divided 2 ½ tablespoons

- Honey 1 tablespoon

- Dry black beans 1 tablespoon

- Dry lentils 1 tablespoon

- Dry kidney beans 1 tablespoon

- Barley 1 tablespoon

- Unbleached 1 cup all-purpose flour

- Whole wheat flour 1 cup

- Millet flour ¼ cup

- Rye flour ¼ cup

- Cracked wheat ¼ cup

- Wheat germ 2 tablespoons

- Salt 1 teaspoon

- Bread machine yeast 2 teaspoons

Instructions

1. In a microwave-safe glass measuring cup, combine milk and water. Microwave on high for 35 seconds. Fill the bread machine halfway with the ingredients. Combine the egg, 2 tsp oil, & honey in a mixing bowl.

2. Finely ground black beans, kidney beans, lentils, and barley in a coffee grinder. In the bread machine, combine the grinds, unbleached flour, whole wheat flour, cracked wheat, millet flour, rye flour, wheat germ, and salt. Toss in the yeast.

3. Start the dough cycle in the bread maker.

4. When the bread machine sounds, remove the dough and punch it down. Roll out the dough with the remaining olive oil on a pastry towel oil a loaf pan. Form the dough in a loaf and lay it in the pan that has been prepared. Cover with a wet towel and let rise for approximately 40 minutes or doubled in volume.

5. Preheat the oven to 375 degrees Fahrenheit (190 degrees C).

6. Uncover the dough and bake for 10 minutes in a preheated oven. Reduce oven temperature to 350 ° F (175 degrees C) and bake for another 30 to 35 minutes, or until golden. Remove the bread from the pan and set it aside to cool for 10 minutes before slicing.

Nutritional values

Calories: 192 kcal | Proteins: 6.6 g | Fats: 5 g | Carbs: 31.5 g

4.22 High Flavor Bran Bread

Prep time: 20 mins

Cook time: 35 mins

Servings: 15

Ingredients

- Warm water 1 ½ cups (110 degrees F/45 degrees C)

- Dry milk powder 2 tablespoons

- Vegetable oil 2 tablespoons

- Molasses 2 tablespoons

- Honey 2 tablespoons

- Salt 1 ½ teaspoons

- Whole wheat flour 2 ¼ cups

- Bread flour 1 ¼ cups

- Whole bran cereal 1 cup

- Active dry yeast 2 teaspoons

Instructions

1. Put ingredients in order suggested by your manufacturer. Choose the whole grain or whole wheat setting.

Nutritional values

Calories: 146 kcal | Proteins: 4.6 g | Fats: 2.4 g | Carbs: 27.9 g

4.23 Sourdough Wheat Bread

Prep time: 5 mins

Cook time: 3 hrs.

Servings: 12

Ingredients

- Sourdough starter 1 ½ cups

- Warm water ⅓ cup (110 degrees f/45 degrees c)

- Margarine 1 ½ tablespoons

- White sugar 1 ½ tablespoons

- Salt ¾ teaspoon

- Whole wheat flour ¾ cup

- All-purpose flour 3 cups

- Active dry yeast 1 ½ teaspoons

Instructions

1. Place all ingredients in the order recommended by your manufacturer. Choose a whole-wheat setting.

Nutritional values

Calories: 203 kcal | Proteins: 6.5 g | Fats: 2 g | Carbs: 39.8 g

4.24 Oat Wheat Bread

Prep time: 10 mins

Cook time: 3 hrs.

Servings: 10

Ingredients

- Whole wheat flour 1 ½ cups

- All-purpose flour 1 cup

- Oat flour ½ cup

- Active dry yeast 2 ½ teaspoons

- Warm water 1 cup

- White sugar 2 tablespoons

- Butter 2 tablespoons

- Salt ½ teaspoon

Instructions

1. Combine the all-purpose flour, whole wheat flour, and oat flour in a mixing bowl and stir well. Stir together the yeast, warm water, and sugar in a separate dish until the sugar has dissolved, then set aside for 10 minutes until a layer of foam develops on top.

2. Put the yeast mixture into the bread machine's pan, then sprinkle the flour mixture on top. Put the butter on one side of the pan and the salt on the other (flour mixture is in the center). Turn on the machine and choose the White Bread setting and the Normal time.

3. Let the bread cool on a wire rack before slicing.

Nutritional values

Calories: 158 kcal | Proteins: 4.8 g | Fats: 3.3 g | Carbs: 28.7 g

4.25 Steve's Whole Wheat

Prep time: 5 mins

Cook time: 3 hrs.

Servings: 12

Ingredients

- Water 1 ⅓ cups
- Dry milk powder 1 ½ tablespoons
- Molasses 1 tablespoon
- Honey 1 tablespoon
- Margarine 3 tablespoons
- White sugar 1 teaspoon
- Salt 1 teaspoon
- Rye flour ½ cup
- Whole wheat flour 2 cups
- Bread flour 1 cup
- Active dry yeast 2 ¾ teaspoons

Instructions

1. Put the ingredients in the manufacturer's suggested sequence in the bread machine pan. Start with the Whole Wheat setting.

Nutritional values

Calories: 166 kcal | Proteins: 5.2 g | Fats: 3.3 g | Carbs: 30.1 g

4.26 Crunchy Wheat and Rye

Prep time: 5 mins

Cook time: 3 hrs.

Servings: 12

Ingredients

- Water 1 ⅓ cups
- Honey 2 tablespoons

- Butter softened 3 tablespoons

- Bread flour 1 cup

- Whole wheat flour 2 cups

- Rye flour ½ cup

- Dry milk powder 1 ½ tablespoons

- Brown sugar 3 tablespoons

- Salt 1 teaspoon

- Bread machine yeast 2 teaspoons

- Wheat and barley ½ cup nugget cereal

Instructions

1. Put the ingredients in the manufacturer's suggested sequence in the bread machine pan. Start with the Whole Wheat setting.

Nutritional values

Calories: 196 kcal | Proteins: 5.7 g | Fats: 3.6 g | Carbs: 36.9 g

4.27 Honey Whole Wheat Bread

Prep time: 5 mins

Cook time: 3 hrs.

Servings: 10

Ingredients

- Warm water 1 ⅛ cups (110 degrees F/45 degrees C)

- Honey 3 tablespoons

- Salt ⅓ teaspoon

- Whole wheat flour 1 ½ cups

- Bread flour 1 ½ cups

- Vegetable oil 2 tablespoons

- Active dry yeast 1 ½ teaspoons

Instructions

1. Toss the ingredients into your bread machine according to the manufacturer's instructions. Use the light color

setting and the wheat bread cycle.

Nutritional values

Calories: 180 kcal | Proteins: 5.2 g | Fats: 3.5 g | Carbs: 33.4 g

Chapter 5: Fruit Bread Recipes

5.1 Fresh fruit bread

Prep time: 15 mins

Cook time: 1 hour

Servings: 2

Ingredients

- Butter ¾ cup

- Sugar 1 ¼ cups

- Eggs 3

- Sour cream 8 ounces

- Vanilla 1 tsp

- Flour 3 cups

- Baking powder ¾ tsp

- Baking soda ½ tsp

- Salt ¾ tsp

- Cinnamon ½ tsp

- Blueberries 2 cups

Instructions

1. Add sour cream, eggs, and vanilla. Add flour, baking soda, baking powder, salt, and cinnamon to the above mixture.

2. Fold in fruit gently.

3. Bake for an hour at 350° in two prepared bread pans.

Nutritional values

Calories: 123 kcal | Proteins: 3 g | Fats: 2 g | Carbs: 21 g

5.2 Spiced fruit loaf

Prep time: 30 mins

Cook time: 20 mins

Servings: 4

Ingredients

For dough

- White flour 450g, for dusting

- Sachets 2 x 7g easy-blend yeast

- Caster sugar 50g

- Warm milk 150ml

- Egg 1, beaten

- Butter 50g unsalted, melted, for greasing

- For greasing oil

For spices

- Ground cinnamon 1½ tsp

- Ground ginger 1 tsp

For dried fruit

- Dried apricot 50g, chopped

- Dried fig 50g, chopped

- Pitted date 50g, chopped

- Sultana 50g

- Cherry 50g, chopped

- 1 orange juice

Instructions

1. Soak the fruit in the orange juice for about 30 minutes, then filter.

2. A big mixing bowl with spices and soaked fruit. Fill the well with heated milk, conserved orange juice, beaten egg, and melted butter. Mix everything with a wooden spoon, then with your hands. If the dough is just too dry, add more warm water or flour.

3. Knead until the dough is smooth and springy. Lid with a clean, moist tea towel. Place in a warm location to rise for 1 hour, depending on the temperature.

4. Rebound the dough by kneading briefly. Flour 2 x 2lb loaf tins. Dough in half. Form each part into a flat oval with a little flour, then the tins. Cover both with a damp cloth and let to prove for 20 minutes. Preheat oven to 180°C/160°F fan/gas 4

5. 20 minutes, cool in tins, turn out, and slice.

Nutritional values

Calories: 190 kcal | Proteins: 5 g | Fats: 4 g | Carbs: 36 g

5.3 Rich fruit loaf

Prep time: 5 mins

Cook time: 30 mins

Servings: 3

Ingredients

- Mixed spice 2 tsp

- Plain flour 3 1/4 cups

- Dried yeast 2 tsp, instant

- Caster sugar 1/4 cup

- Warm water 1 1/2 cups

- Dried dates 1/2 cup, chopped

- Sultanas 1/3 cup

- Currants 1/3 cup

- Diced apricots 1/3 cup

- Dried figs 1/2 cup, quartered

- Milk 2 tsp

- Cinnamon sugar 1 tbsp

- To serve, butter

- To serve, jam

Instructions

1. Sift the 3 cups flour and mixed spice. Add yeast and sugar. Make a hole in the middle. Fill with water. To make a soft dough. Turn onto a floured surface. Remaining flour Knead about 10 minutes, or until smooth.

2. Preheat oven to 350°F (180°C). Cover with oiled plastic wrap. Wait an hour or until it doubles in size. Preheat oven to 180°C/gas mark 6.

3. Punch the dough with your fist. Knead for a while. Turn onto a floured surface. Add dates, sultanas, currants, and apricots gradually. Make a log of 25cm round of dough figs on top. In a pan, prepare. Cover with oiled plastic wrap. Set aside for fifteen min or till the dough reaches the pan's rim.

4. Preheat oven to 200C/180C fan-forced. Milk the top of the dough. Cinnamon sugar sprinkling 10 min. Baking Reduce oven to 170°C/150°C fan-forced. Bake for 30 minutes, or till golden brown & hollow. 5 minutes in the pan Place on a wire rack until cool. Butter and jam on toast

Nutritional values

Calories: 146 kcal | Proteins: 6 g | Fats: 4 g | Carbs: 31 g

5.4 Fruit Bread

Prep time: 3 hours

Cook time: 45 mins

Servings: 4

Ingredients

- Flour, whole wheat 2.5 cups

- All-purpose flour ½ cup

- Regular sugar 5 tablespoon

- Active yeast ½ tablespoon

- Custard Powder 2 tablespoon

- Salt 1 teaspoon

- Water 1 cup
- Tutti Frutti 2 tablespoon
- Orange peels 2.5 tablespoons, chopped
- Glazed cherries 3 to 4, chopped
- Vegetable oil 4 tablespoon

Instructions

1. Warm the water.
2. Stir in a pinch of sugar.
3. Add dried active yeast.
4. Keep heated for 10 minutes to froth yeast.
5. Toss both flours in a separate bowl with tutti frutti, cherries, candied orange peel, custard powder/corn starch.
6. Mix in the yeast and oil to form a smooth dough.
7. Rehydrate the driest dough.
8. Grease the dough with oil to prevent it from drying out.
9. Same bowl.
10. Just let the dough rise for 2–2 1/2 hours, covered with cling film or a kitchen towel.
11. After 2 or 2 1/2 hours, punch and knead lightly.
12. a 9x4 inch loaf pan
13. Make a loaf of dough.
14. Cover and let rise for 35-45 minutes.
15. Preheat the oven to 180°C/356°F before baking.
16. 45-50 minutes bake
17. Remove when hot and place on a wired tray/stand.
18. Serve hot or cold.
19. It goes well with tea or coffee.
20. You could even apply vegan or dairy butter and eat them.

Nutritional values

Calories: 2348 kcal | Proteins: 49 g | Fats: 66 g | Carbs: 411 g

5.5 Christmas Fruit Bread Wreath

Prep time: 30 mins

Cook time: 30 mins

Servings: 2

Ingredients

- Flour 8 cups, approximately
- Instant yeast 1 package, about a tbsp
- Sugar 1/2 cup
- Salt 1 tsp
- Vanilla extract 2 tsp
- Melted butter ½ cup
- Warm milk 2 cups
- Eggs 2
- Glacé fruit 1 ½ cups
- Glacé cherries 1 cup, cut into quarters

Instructions

1. In a large bowl or the dough hook of an electric mixer, combine 3 cups flour, instant yeast, sugar, and salt.

2. Eggs, vanilla essence, and melted butter

3. Mix for 4-5 minutes with a wooden spoon or even the usual paddle of the electric mixer until smooth and lump-free.

4. Using an immersion blender, turn to the dough hook and gradually add the remaining flour. If you don't have an electric mixer, try mixing with flour till a soft dough develops and exits the bowl. It's normal to use less or more flour than called for in the recipe.

5. Extra 10 minutes in the immersion blender or even on a dusted breadboard and countertop. Cover the dough and let it sit for 15 minutes.

6. Punch the dough down and hand knead in the combined fruit and chopped cherries.

7. Split the dough into three equal halves to form a wreath and roll each into an 18-inch strand.

8. Form a circle by tucking one side of the dough under another and squeezing the ends together.

9. Preheat oven to 350°F. Wrap with a clean tea towel and then let rise for 2 hours. (At this point, you can egg wash it to help it brown. The egg wash is made by whisking 1 egg & 1 tbsp water together.

10. Bake for 25-30 minutes 350°F until golden brown.

11. Divide dough into 3 parts and shape into straight loaves and 3 bun loaves as desired. Bake loaves for 35-40 minutes.

Nutritional values

Calories: 181 kcal | Proteins: 5 g | Fats: 4 g | Carbs: 31 g

5.6 Cinnamon and Raisin Fruit Loaf

Prep time: 15 mins

Cook time: 1 hour

Servings: 2

Ingredients

- Dried cherries 30g

- Raisins & golden sultanas 125g mixed

- Apricots 50g dried, finely chopped

- Lady Grey tea 250ml, cold

- White bread flour 400g strong

- (2 tsp) 7g sachet active dried yeast

- Cinnamon 1 tsp ground

- Caster sugar 2 tbsp

- Salt ½ tsp

- 1 orange, grated zest

- Butter 55g, melted & cooled slightly

- Egg 1 medium, beaten

- Full-fat milk 150ml, warmed

- For greasing oil

Instructions

1. Pour the tea over the fruit and let it simmer for just a couple of hours until draining well.

2. Mix the flour, yeast, sugar, cinnamon, salt, and orange zest in a large bowl. Make it into the center. Pour the egg, butter, and milk into the well inside the flour mixture. Mix with a wooden spoon. Add the fruit to the dough just before it comes together.

3. The dough should be elastic and smooth after ten minutes of kneading on a frivolously floured surface. Make sure to keep the dough warm and covered with oiled cling film for 30 minutes or doubled in size.

4. Punch the dough gently and transfer it to something like a lightly floured. Form the dough into an oblong or circle and place in a 900g loaf tin. Wrap with oiled cling film and set to double in size for 30 minutes.

5. 200°C/fan180°C/gas 6 Brush the bread in melted butter and sprinkle with sugar. Bake for 25 minutes, or until the topping is golden brown and the loaf sounds hollow when tapped. Cool on a grate.

Nutritional values

Calories: 292 kcal | Proteins: 7.4 g | Fats: 7.7 g | Carbs: 51.5 g

5.7 Eggnog Fruit Bread

Prep time: 25 mins

Cook time: 1 hour

Servings: 2

Ingredients

- Eggs 3 large, room temperature

- Vegetable oil 1 cup

- Sugar 1-1/2 cups

- Vanilla extract 3/4 teaspoon

- Rum extract 3/4 teaspoon

- Eggnog 1-1/2 cups

- Flour 3 cups, divided

- Baking powder 2 teaspoons

- Salt 1/2 teaspoon

- Ground nutmeg 1/2 teaspoon

- Candied fruit 1 cup

- Chopped walnuts 1/2 cup

Instructions

1. **Combine eggs with oil, 2 1/2 cups flour, sugar, extracts, eggnog, salt, baking powder, and nutmeg. Mix in the remaining flour with the fruit. Add walnuts.**

2. **Place 8 x 4-inch buttered loaf pans for 65-70 minutes at 350°F till a toothpick comes away clean. Remove from pans onto a wire rack to cool fully.**

Nutritional values

Calories: 186 kcal | Proteins: 0.5 g | Fats: 2 g | Carbs: 31 g

5.8 Luxury Fruit Bread

Prep time: 2 hours

Cook time: 25 mins

Servings: 1

Ingredients

For Yeast Batter

- 100grams, White Bread Flour

- 5grams Yeast

- 1tsp Sugar

- Milk (Lukewarm) – 250ml

For the Dough

- 350grams White Bread Flour

- 50grams Unsalted Butter

- 50grams Sugar

- ½tsp Salt

- 25grams Cashew Nuts

- 25 grams Pistachio

- 25 grams Almonds

- 25 grams Walnuts

- 25grams Raisins

- 25grams Sultanas

- Cranberries, Dried Apple – 25grams

- 25grams, Chopped Dates

- ½tsp Cinnamon Powder

- 1 Egg

Instructions

1. Toss in all nuts & dried fruits (excluding raisins and sultanas).

2. Beneath the yeast batter is flour, yeast, and Lastly, beat inside this milk until smooth.

3. Wrap in foil and let foam for 20 minutes.

4. Separately, combine flour and salt. Add the butter.

5. Fruits and cinnamon powder mix.

6. Eggs beaten Add to yeast batter. Stir in the flour and fruit. Mix thoroughly with a spatula.

7. Knead the dough, adding flour as needed until smooth and thus no longer sticky.

8. Wrap in foil and let it rise for 50-60 minutes in a warm area until twice in size.

9. Unbuttoned 9kg loaves Disperse the dough. Don't squish. Fill only 3/4 full since it will rise.

10. Preheat oven to 200C/400F/Gas Mark 6. Bake for 20 minutes in the oven.

11. Cook for another 25 minutes, loosely covered with foil. Pour some water on top of the bread and bake for 30 minutes. If the skewer comes with damp dough, add 10-15 minutes.

12. Take out of the oven. Cool fully. Serve sliced. Serve with Coffee or Tea.

Nutritional values

Calories: 178 kcal | Proteins: 0.2 g | Fats: 3 g | Carbs: 35 g

5.9 Leftover Fruit Bread

Prep time: 2 hours

Cook time: 15 mins

Servings: 8

Ingredients

- Cooking spray Nonstick for the loaf pan
- Banana 1 overripe
- Sugar 2/3 cup
- Butter 8 tablespoons, cooled & melted
- Greek yogurt 1/2 cup
- Orange juice 1 tablespoon
- Vanilla extract 1 teaspoon
- Egg 1 large
- Baking soda 1 teaspoon
- Kosher salt 1/2 teaspoon
- All-purpose flour 1 1/2 cups
- Ripe peaches 1 cup diced
- Blueberries 1 cup

Instructions

1. Preheat oven to 350°F. Grease a 9-by-5-inch loaf pan. Spray the overhanging parchment with cooking spray.

2. In a medium bowl, mash the banana. Whisk in the yogurt, vanilla, orange juice, and egg.

3. 1 1/2 cups flour, baking soda, salt by using a spatula, fold in the dry ingredients. Fold in the peaches & blueberries with the additional 2 tablespoons of flour. Pour batter into pan.

4. Bake for 50 minutes till a toothpick inserted inside the middle comes out clean. After 10 minutes, remove the bread from the pan and cool thoroughly on a rack.

Nutritional values

Calories: 125 kcal | Proteins: 1 g | Fats: 2.6 g | Carbs: 32 g

5.10 Best Holiday Fruitcake

Prep time: 15 mins

Cook time: 2 hours

Servings: 4

Ingredients

- Baking soda 1 teaspoon

- Sour cream 1 cup (236ml)

- Chopped dates 1 cup (130g)

- Raisins 2 cups (280g)

- Glazed cherries ½ cup

- Chopped walnuts 1 cup (100g)

- All-purpose flour 2 cups (260g), divided

- Unsalted butter 8 tablespoons, (113g)

- Sugar 1 cup (200g)

- Egg 1 large

- 1 orange zest, finely grated

- Salt 1 teaspoon

- Brandy 1 to 2 ounces, optional

Instructions

Prep the oven and the pan:

1. 325F (160C) oven preheat Grease a 9 x 5-inch loaf pan. Trim the paper to fit.

2. One-piece should cover half of the pan and be an inch above the rim. Cover the opposite sides with the remaining pieces. After baking, pull the cake out of the pan by gripping the edges of the paper.

Add the Sour cream with baking soda:

3. Mix the Baking soda & sour cream in a small bowl.

Flour the fruits and nuts:

4. mix the 1/4 cup (30g) flour, raisins, dates, cherries, & almonds. Toss Flour the fruit and nuts thoroughly. Set it aside.

Make the batter:

5. Cream butter and sugar till fluffy. Then the egg, orange rind, and sour cream/baking soda.

6. Mix in the leftover 1 3/4 cups (230g) flour & salt. Pour the fruit & nut combination into the batter, then mix well.

Make fruitcake:

7. Pour the batter into a 5 x 9-inch loaf pan and smooth the top.

8. Put the pan in the oven. Place a pan of water inside the oven, either underneath or beside the fruitcake. (The water helps cook evenly and gently.)

9. Bake at 325°F (160°C) for 1 1/2 to 1 3/4 hours, or until a wooden skewer placed into the center comes out clean. If the water evaporates during baking, it must be replaced.

10. If the surface of the fruitcake is browning too quickly, tent it with foil.

Sprinkle with brandy and let cool:

11. Remove from oven and allow for 5 minutes to cool. Then, using the parchment paper's edges, remove the cake to a rack to cool it entirely.

12. To store, wrap in plastic first, then aluminum.

13. Poke a few holes in the cake, then sprinkle with brandy or bourbon. This will keep the fruitcake moist and longer.

Nutritional values

Calories: 320 kcal | Proteins: 4 g | Fats: 13 g | Carbs: 50 g

5.11 Fruit Soda Bread

Prep time: 10 mins

Cook time: 50 mins

Servings: 7

Ingredients

- All-purpose, 1 cup
- Caster sugar 100 g
- Baking powder 2 tsp
- Baking soda 1 tsp
- Juicy raisins 200 g
- Salt 1/4 tsp
- Eggs 2 large
- Buttermilk 250 ml

- Butter 50 g melted

Instructions

1. Bake at 175°C. Sprinkle a baking sheet with flour.

2. Frozen fruit and nuts are added to the batter in a big bowl. Mix it all up. Your dry mix.

3. Pour the eggs into a cup, then beat gently with a fork. Set aside all but 1 tablespoon of the egg. Mix in buttermilk and melted butter. Your wet mix.

4. Pour the wet mix into the dry mix and mix until a sticky dough forms. Don't overmix, or your bread will be tough. Use your hands if you don't feel like getting sticky. Place the dough on the prepared baking sheet in a rough cob or ball form.

5. Make a huge cross in the center of the bread using a sharp knife. Apply an egg wash to the entire loaf with a pastry brush. Bake for 45-50 minutes till the bread is browned.

6. Remove from oven and cool for ten min before slicing or toasting with butter.

Nutritional values

Calories: 243 kcal | Proteins: 5.7 g | Fats: 4.2 g | Carbs: 47 g

5.12 Golden Egg and Dried Fruit

Prep time: 45 mins

Cook time: 30 mins

Servings: 3

Ingredients

- Water ¾ cup - 170 gr

- Eggs 2 large - 50 gr

- Vegetable oil 6 tablespoons - 75 gr

- Granulated sugar ¼ cup - 50 gr

- Sea salt 1 ½ teaspoon - 9 gr

- Dried cherries, dried cranberries ⅔ cup, or raisins

- Bread flour 3 cups unbleached - 360 gr

- Bread machine yeast 2 teaspoons - 6 gr

Instructions

1. Put the ingredients in the bread machine pan. Start the DOUGH cycle. (If preferred, add fruit at the ending of the kneading round.)

2. Lift the cover twice throughout the mixing & kneading stages to check the dough. Examine the paddles for the first time as soon as the machine starts mixing.

3. Check the dough consistency fifteen minutes into the DOUGH cycle. A typical recipe calls for a sticky dough that pulls cleanly away.

4. Too moist dough? Add flour a tbsp at a time.

5. If the dough is just too dry, 1 tablespoon of liquid at such time until it is perfect.

6. If the dough has increased in size after the DOUGH cycle, remove it to a floured surface. If the dough hasn't risen enough, let it rise in the machine before continuing.

7. To form a rectangle, take the dough from the bread machine pan and roll it out slightly longer than the pan. Begin rolling the dough from the long side. Put this roll inside a 9 x 4-inch loaf pan. It should half-fill the pan.

8. Cover loosely with such a paper cloth and let rise until about doubled. (Can take an hour or over.)

9. Pre-heat oven to 350F. Bake for 45 mins or till cooked through golden brown. Wrap with aluminum foil for the last third of cooking time to prevent over-browning. When done, the inside temperature should be 190F.

10. Cool the baked loaf on the countertop for 15 minutes. Place on a cooling rack.

Nutritional values

Calories: 227 kcal | Proteins: 33 g | Fats: 8 g | Carbs: 33 g

5.13 Irish Barmbrack

Prep time: 10 mins

Cook time: 1 hour 20 mins

Servings: 6

Ingredients

- Tea 1 cup
- Golden raisins 3/4 cup
- Dried cranberries 1/2 cup
- Cherries 1/2 cup, dried
- Orange peel 1/2 tsp dried
- Egg 1 large
- Ground cinnamon 1 tsp
- Ground cloves 1/2 tsp
- Ground nutmeg 1/2 tsp
- Light brown sugar 1 cup (packed)
- Self-rising flour 2 cups

Instructions

1. Combine the black brewed tea, dried fruits, plus candied peel (preferably orange zest) in such a bowl and refrigerate overnight.

2. Preheat oven to 350°F (175°C), then butter a 9x5-inch loaf pan.

3. Then add the spices (cinnamon clove nutmeg) or brown sugar to the tea-fruit mixture. Stir in all of the self-rising flour.

4. Mix until all flour is mixed, then transfer to the loaf pan. After 1 hour, examine the color of the baked bread (if it is going too brown, wrap with aluminum foil to keep on from browning too deeply).

5. Bake your bread for 1 hour 15-30 min (mine is typically done at 75-80 minutes). Cool the baked loaf on a wire rack before slicing & serving. Preheat oven to 350°F. Bake for 1 hour.

Nutritional values

Calories: 221 kcal | Proteins: 3 g | Fats: 0.6 g | Carbs: 51 g

5.14 Hearty Barley Fruit Bread

Prep time: 10 mins

Cook time: 50 mins

Servings: 3

Ingredients

- Cooking spray, Nonstick

- Sucanat, 96 g (½ cup)

- Dried figs 149 g (1 cup), chopped

- 80 g raisins, (½ cup)

- Orange peel 3 ounces (85 g), diced candied

- 120 g walnuts (1 cup), coarsely chopped

- Fine sea salt ½ teaspoon

- Ground cinnamon 1 teaspoon

- Grated nutmeg, ¼ teaspoon

- 210 g barley flour, (1¾ cups)

- 16 g arrowroot powder (2 tablespoons)

- Baking powder 2 teaspoons

- 1 cup vegan milk (235 ml)

- Plain vegan yogurt, 120 g

Instructions

1. Preheat oven to 350F (180C, gas). A light cooking spray coating an 8 x 4 inch (20 x 10 cm) bread pan

2. Add orange peel, arrowroot powder, figs, and Sucanat flour/cornstarch, plus baking powder in a big bowl.

3. In a big bowl, Milk and yogurt are combined.

4. Put the wet ingredients over the dry and mix. Then bake for 50 mins., or until golden and firm on top.

5. Set aside on a wire rack. Cool fully before slicing. This bread can keep for a week wrapped in aluminum foil. It freezes well too.

Nutritional values

Calories: 237 kcal | Proteins: 7 g | Fats: 3 g | Carbs: 48 g

5.15 Authentic Hutzelbrot

Prep time: 1 hour 30 mins

Cook time: 1 hour

Servings: 5

Ingredients

- Dried pears 16 ounces

- Dried figs 12 ounces

- 8 ounces dried apricots (250 grams)

- 8 ounces dried plums (250 grams)

- 4 cups water (950 ml)

- 16 ounces raisins (500 grams)

- Rum 3 tablespoons

- Active yeast 3 teaspoons

- 2 1/2 cups flour (350 grams)

- 1 1/2 cups dark rye flour (150 grams)

- 3/4 cup granulated sugar (150 grams)

- Salt 1/4 teaspoon

- Ground cinnamon 2 tablespoons

- Crushed anise seed 1 1/2 tablespoons

- Whole hazelnuts 8 ounces

- Whole almonds 8 ounces

- Orange peel 2 ounces

- Lemon peel 2 ounces

- Lemon peel & candied orange

- One lemon zest

- Blanched almonds 16 whole

Instructions

1. Pour water over the dry fruits (excluding the raisins). Bring to a boil, then reduce to a boil for 15 minutes. Turn the heat down for 3 hours. Pour the liquid into a colander more than a dish. Strain it for long enough to get rid of as much liquid as possible. Save the fruit liquid for later. Whereas the dried fruits cool, combine the raisins and rum in a bowl.

2. Toast whole almonds & hazelnuts until fragrant, then cut coarsely after chilled (preferably just in half). Chop the dried fruits coarsely.

3. Mix in the yeast and a few teaspoons of sugar. Allow mixture to settle for 15 minutes until frothy.

4. Whereas the yeast mixture rests, combine the flours, salt, sugar, ground anise seed, and cinnamon in a stand mixer bowl. Fill the well with the yeast mixture. Using a dough hook, mix the mixture for 6 minutes until it comes together. It will be quite solid. Re-spray the bowl and replace the dough ball. Cover it loosely with plastic wrap & set it aside for 30 minutes. The dough will very barely puff up.

5. Mix the chopped dried fruits and raisins with the candied orange peels and lemon and roasted nuts. Knead the mixture with the dough hook until well combined. The dried fruits get mushier and integrate into the dough, which may be rather wet based on how much liquid was removed from them. Continue to add flour till the dough is controllable. It must be soft, moist, and not too wet. Reduce the moisture until the dough is workable to roll out onto a worktop and add flour as needed.

6. Lay the dough out on a well-floured surface. Using your hands, knead the dough until it's soft, flexible, and not sticky on the exterior.

7. Into a large, lightly sprayed bowl, place the dough ball. Rest it for 2 hours at room temperature. It will only rise a little, becoming puffy. Refrigerate it overnight, punching it up in the center. This will enhance the yeast dough's flavor and allow the flavors of the fruits & spices to infiltrate the dough thoroughly.

8. If in a hurry, omit the overnight refrigeration stage (though we recommend it). After 2 hours of resting at room temperature, form the Hutzelbrot loaves, rest for 60-90 minutes till slightly puffy, brush with fruit juice, and bake as directed.

9. 4-5 hours at room temperature after refrigerating the dough the day before. It won't rise much, but it will puff

up. Cut the dough into 4 equal sections (even if it hasn't risen much, it'll be fluffy when cut). Make the loaves smaller so the inside bakes entirely well before the outside burns.

10. Place the oval-shaped loaves on a prepared baking sheet. NOTE: You may also divide them into 8 smaller loaves (It is recommended to make them into these little round loaves), then bake them for less time.

11. Place the whole roasted almonds on top as usual (see pictures). Location the loaves in a hot environment for 60-90 minutes, until somewhat puffy.

12. Preheat oven to 350°F.

13. Brush the saved fruit juice all over each loaf, storing half for later. Bake for an hour on the center rack, till very dark brown but just not burned. Pick one up and tap on the bottom with a dish towel to see whether it's hollow.

14. Take the loaves from the oven and brush them over with the leftover fruit juice while still hot. Let them cool slightly before wrapping securely in plastic wrap, then foil to "ripen" for several days (traditionally 2 weeks in a cool environment). For the greatest flavor and texture. If you plan to age them for a few days, you can put them in the fridge, but they will harden. To soften the slices, microwave them for a few seconds.

15. Slice, butter, and enjoy.

Nutritional values

Calories: 206 kcal | Proteins: 3 g | Fats: 5 g | Carbs: 38 g

5.16 Tea loaf

Prep time: 2 hours

Cook time: 30 mins

Servings: 1

Ingredients

- Bread flour 400g/14oz, for dusting

- Salt 1 ½ tsp

- Caster sugar 1 ½ oz.

- Butter 1 ½ oz.

- Dried yeast ¼ oz.

- Milk 120 ml

- Sultanas 1 ¾ oz.

- Glace cherries 2 ¼ oz.

- Cinnamon 1 tsp ground

- Zest of 3 oranges

Instructions

1. Mix the flour, sugar, salt, butter, milk, yeast, and 120ml/4fl oz water.

2. Pour the dough onto a lightly floured surface and knead till smooth and flexible.

3. Put the dough in a bowl and let it rest for just an hour.

4. Work in the sultanas, cherries, cinnamon, and orange zest with an electric mixer or your hands.

5. Flatten the dough, then roll it up into a sausage form.

6. Grease a baking sheet with butter. To shield the dough against drafts, put the baking tray on the inside of a plastic bag, trying to avoid touching the loaf's top. Let stand for an hour.

7. Prepare 220C/425F/Gas 7 oven.

8. Bake for 25-30 mins, then cool on a wire rack.

9. Make water icing while the loaf cools. Combine the icing sugar with the water to produce a paste in a bowl. Add more water till the icing coats the wooden spoon.

10. Drizzle or put frosting on the tea bread. Slice and enjoy with lots of butter.

Nutritional values

Calories: 265 kcal | Proteins: 4 g | Fats: 0.6 g | Carbs: 33 g

5.17 Strawberry Bread

Prep time: 10 mins

Cook time: 50 mins

Servings: 2

Ingredients

For the Bread

- Granulated sugar 3/4 cup

- Milk 1/2 cup

- Oil 1/2 cup

- Egg 1 large

- Vanilla extract 1 teaspoon

- 2 cups flour, all-purpose

- Baking powder, 2 teaspoons

- Salt 1/4 teaspoon

- Diced strawberries 2 cups

- All-purpose flour, 2 tablespoons

For the Glaze

- Powdered sugar 2 cups

- Melted butter 2 tablespoons

- 1/3 cup strawberries, finely diced

- Vanilla extract, 1/2 teaspoon

- Heavy cream 1-2 tablespoons

Instructions

1. Preheat oven to 350°F.

2. Add sugar, oil, milk, egg, and vanilla in a medium bowl. Separately, mix flour, baking powder, then salt. Mix the dry and wet ingredients until just mixed.

3. Toss the strawberries with the 2 tablespoons flour in a small bowl. Gently fold in the floured strawberries.

4. Then pour the batter into an oiled 9"x5" pan. Bake for 50-55 minutes at 350°F. Unblemished toothpick put in the center of the bread. After 10 minutes, transfer the loaf to a wire rack to dry fully.

5. Combine powdered sugar, diced strawberries, melted butter, and extract in a small bowl. Blend until smooth.

6. After the bread has cooled, glaze it. Serve sliced.

Nutritional values

Calories: 394 kcal | Proteins: 4 g | Fats: 14 g | Carbs: 62 g

5.18 Fruit and Nut Sourdough Bread

Prep time: 1 hour

Cook time: 7 hours 5 mins

Servings: 1

Ingredients

- **Sourdough starter** 80 grams

- **All-purpose flour**, 200 grams (1 + 2/3 cups)

- **Whole wheat flour** 200 grams (1 + 2/3 cups)

- **Water** 260 grams

- **Salt** 8 grams

- **Dried figs**, 1/3 cup chopped

- **Raisins** 1/4 cup

- **Walnuts** 1/4 cup

- **Pepitas** 2 tablespoons **(pumpkin seeds)**

- **Sunflower seeds** 2 tablespoons

Instructions

1. Prepare the starter: if the sourdough starter isn't ready, feed it 12 hours ahead of time. Add 50 g all-purpose flour & 50 g water to the old starter. Allow it to double in size for 6 hours.

2. Pour a tablespoon of fresh starters into a glass of warm water. If it floats, it's ready. You can either let it sit longer to create more bubbles or feed it after 6–12 hours to pass the float test.

3. Get the dough:

4. In a large mixing bowl, combine sourdough starter, whole wheat flour, all-purpose flour, and water (there should be not too dry flour particles visible). Just let the dough rest for thirty min. The rest period increases bulk yeast development and enables the dough to build gluten strength without kneading organically.

5. Add salt and mix for a few seconds. Because salt inhibits yeast growth, it is best to add it after the dough has rested for 30 minutes.

6. Build the gluten connection in the dough: because it is 68 percent hydrated, it is less sticky and holds its shape better. So, either make the dough by hand or stretch & fold it:

7. Hand kneads the dough: place the dough on a dry surface. Use your palms to press the dough down then outward. Fold the dough in halves and press. For 5 minutes, push the bread down and forth, then fold it in towards you. Take the dough and slam it into the counter, then fold it towards you. (slap and fold kneading technique) let the dough rest for 5 minutes with a big bowl upside fell on top. Resting dough causes gluten to relax and strengthen more efficiently. Knead the dough for 5 minutes more until it is soft and supple. A very well dough is soft and firm. If you poke the dough with your thumb, the depression should bounce back. If it doesn't rebound but remains a dimple, keep kneading. Refrigerate the dough for 2.5 hours or until it doubles in size.

8. Stretch, then fold the dough in the dish by bringing the edges over to the middle, one at a time. If you use wet hands, folding all four sides should take less than a minute. Let the dough stand for 30 minutes. Replenish stretching and folding the dough for 30 minutes. Stretch or fold the dough one last time, cover it, and let it rest for 90 minutes or until it approximately doubles in size.

9. Shape the dough and add fruit:

10. Mix inside the dried figs, raisins, and walnuts. Make sure all dried fruit is uniformly distributed throughout the dough.

11. Move dough to a floured surface. Fold the edges of the dough into the middle to form a compact ball. Knead the dough some and fold all four aspects in towards the middle. Turn dough over to use your table scraper to form a tight ball. Rep till the dough becomes tight.

12. In a small bowl, add pepitas and sunflower seeds. Dampen the dough by gently rubbing it on a damp dishcloth before dipping it in the seeds. Scatter seeds over the dough.

13. Dough proof:

14. A clean dishcloth lines a 7-inch-diameter bowl. Flour the dishcloth well, so the dough doesn't stick. Place the seeded piece down into the lined bowl (or into a proofing basket). Cover the bowl with a lid or a cloth to keep the dough moist.

15. Rest the dough at room temperature for 3–3.5 hours (or shift the bowl into the fridge and let the dough cool all night for 8-12 hrs).

16. Scoring dough:

17. Take the bowl from the fridge and lay it in the middle of a 9x9 parchment paper.

18. So because the dough is coated in seeds, delicately clip the dough with scissors. Make no deeper cuts than 1/2 inch.

19. To reassemble, re-place the dough in the same bowl and cover it with a towel while the oven is hot. A few minutes before baking, keep the dough in the bowl.

20. Preheat oven to 450°f and put a 4-quart dutch oven (or a 9-inch oven-safe cooking pot) with a metal lid in the oven. Bake in dutch ovens. They retain heat better than ordinary cookware.

21. Place the parchment paper, then dough into the prepared dutch oven. Bake 30 minutes with the lid on.

22. After 30 minutes, replace the lid and bake the bread open for 20 minutes.

23. Remove the parchment paper and the bread from the dutch oven. Let the bread cool entirely on a rack for an hour. To confirm if the bread is done, tap it on the bottom with your finger. When done, the bread will be hollow.

Nutritional values

Calories: 166 kcal | Proteins: 5.3 g | Fats: 2.1 g | Carbs: 33 g

5.19 No-Knead Harvest Bread

Prep time: 15 mins

Cook time: 1 hour

Servings: 2

Ingredients

- Salt 2 teaspoons

- Whole wheat flour 1 cup

- Bread flour 3 ¼ cups

- Instant yeast 1/2 teaspoon

- Cool water 1 3/4 cups (397g)

- Dried cranberries 3/4 cup

- Golden raisins 1/2 cup (85g)

- Walnuts 1 cup (113g)

Instructions

1. Pour flour into a cup and whisk off any excess. Mix flours, salt, yeast, and water in a large bowl. Then, using your hands, pull the dough ball together, adding all the flour.

2. Include fruits and nuts.

3. The dough will become frothy and rise a lot, so use a big bowl.

4. Then shape the dough into a log round or loaf to fit your 14- to 15-inch lidded stoneware baker, 9-inch x 12-inch oval deep casserole pan with cover, or 9- to 10-inch round covered baking crock.

5. Place the dough, smooth side up, in the prepared pan.

6. Cover and let it rise for 2 hours at room temperature. It should rise significantly, but not dramatically.

7. Crosshatch the bread with a sharp knife or lame. Put the butter in the oven broiler with the cover on. Preheat oven to 450°F and bake bread.

8. Bake for 45-50 minutes (begin the timer whenever you put the bread into the cold oven). Remove the lid and bake for 5–15 minutes more until it's deep brown and a digital thermometer placed in the center reads 205°F.

9. Take the bread from the oven cool thoroughly before slicing.

10. Keep the bread wrapped well at room temp for a few days; freeze for longer.

Nutritional values

Calories: 196 kcal | Proteins: 7 g | Fats: 5 g | Carbs: 33 g

5.20 Light Fruit Cake Loaf

Prep time: 30 mins

Cook time: 1 hour 5 mins

Servings: 4

Ingredients

- 185g spread, low fat

- Caster sugar 115g

- Eggs 4, beaten

- Self-raising flour 185g

- Flour 60g, plain

- Dried fruit 260g mixed

- Apricots 60g dried, chopped

- Cherries 100g glace, halved

- Milk 125ml

Instructions

1. Bake at 160C/315F/Gas 3. Grease or line a loaf pan with butter or spread.

2. In a big bowl, beat spread with caster sugar till pale and fluffy.

3. Beat the eggs, then mix in the flour, fruits, and milk.

4. Bake for 80-90 minutes, or until a skewer pierced comes out clean.

5. After 15 minutes, remove the tin and cool fully on the wire rack.

Nutritional values

Calories: 196 kcal | Proteins: 8 g | Fats: 0.5 g | Carbs: 51 g

5.21 Fruit And Spice Soda Bread

Prep time: 30 mins

Cook time: 35 mins

Servings: 3

Ingredients

- Rolled porridge oat 100g

- Butter 25g, diced

- Plain flour 200g

- Wholemeal flour 200g

- Caster sugar 100g

- Bicarbonate of soda 1 tsp

- Mixed spice 1 ½ tsp

- Raisin 50g

- Sultana 50g

- Stoned date 50g, finely chopped

- Mixed peel 3 tbsp

- Buttermilk 450ml

- Demerara sugar 3-4 tbsp

Instructions

1. Turn on the oven at 180°C fan/gas 6. Rub the butter into the porridge oats with your fingertips in a large bowl. Add 1 tsp salt, raisins, sultanas, dates, and mixed peel

2. Stir in the buttermilk with the round knife. Pour out onto a floured board and carefully roll into a ball. Put to a flour-dusted baking tray & sprinkle with demerara sugar. Cut a huge cross in the top with a flour-dusted knife and bake until crispy for 30-35 minutes. Warm or cold, with butter.

Nutritional values

Calories: 405 kcal | Proteins: 10 g | Fats: 5 g | Carbs: 79 g

5.22 Low Sugar Bread with Dried Fruit And Nuts

Prep time: 15 mins

Cook time: 45 mins

Servings: 2

Ingredients

- Plain yogurt 1 1/4 cups

- Eggs 2 large

- Sunflower oil 3 tablespoons

- Vanilla extract 1 teaspoon

- Dried fruit 2/3 cup

- Chopped nuts 1 cup

- 2 cups flour, self-rising

- Granulated sugar, 1/2 cup

- Baking powder 1 teaspoon

Instructions

1. Preheat the oven to 350F

2. Butter the inside of a loaf pan before baking. Cover the pan with foil paper that fits around the edges.

3. Put the paper in. Set it aside.

4. Pour the plain yogurt into a medium bowl.

5. A fork-mixed egg in a mixing bowl Mix in the sunflower oil or vanilla using a fork.

6. Dry ingredients: sugar, flour, baking powder.

7. Stir the yogurt mix into the flour.

8. Mix all ingredients using a spatula or even a spoon. Fill the prepared baking pan with the mixture.

9. Bake for 45 minutes or till golden and risen. Skewer or toothpick the bread to test it. It should be fine.

10. Remove the bread from the pan by removing the parchment paper ends.

Nutritional values

Calories: 174 kcal | Proteins: 5 g | Fats: 8 g | Carbs: 21 g

5.23 Sultana Loaf

Prep time: 20 mins

Cook time: 1 hour

Servings: 3

Ingredients

- 1 Cup Raisins, 130 grams
- Butter 30 grams, diced
- Baking Soda 1 teaspoon
- Boiling Water 1 Cup, 250 MLS
- Sugar 1 Cup, 205 grams
- White Flour 2 Cups, 260 grams
- Baking Powder 1 teaspoon
- Cinnamon Powder 1 teaspoon
- Salt, a Pinch

- Egg 1, Well Beaten

- Golden Syrup 1 Tablespoon, 15 ml

- Vanilla Essence 1 teaspoon, 5 ml

Instructions

1. Preheat oven to 180C.

2. Prepare a loaf pan with baking paper.

3. Cook for 3-5 minutes, occasionally stirring, with the Sultanas (or raisins), baking soda, butter, and boiling water.

4. Remove from heat, pour into a large bowl, chill for 5-10 minutes, or refrigerate.

5. Stir in the sugar, baking powder, flour, cinnamon, and salt.

6. Then add an egg, golden syrup, and vanilla.

7. Combine all ingredients until no flour remains.

8. Bake for an hour in the prepared loaf pan. A skewer and knife inserted into the loaf come out clean, with moist crumbs but no batter.

9. After baking, remove the bread from the pan and cool on a wire rack for 20 minutes.

10. Keep chilled for 4 days in an airtight container.

11. This loaf can be stored whole or cut and frozen.

12. Serve plain or with margarine.

13. Enjoy.

Nutritional values

Calories: 289 kcal | Proteins: 0.9 g | Fats: 2 g | Carbs: 56 g

5.24 All-Bran Fruit Loaf Recipe

Prep time: 30 mins

Cook time: 1 hour 10 mins

Servings: 4

Ingredients

- For greasing, margarine

- Self-raising flour, 100g

- Skimmed milk 300ml

- Dried fruit 275g mixed

- Caster sugar 150g

- All-bran 100g, original

Instructions

1. Preheat oven to 180°C (gas mark 4).

2. Combine Kellogg's All-Bran, sugar, and dried fruit in a large bowl.

3. Mix in milk and let stand for 30 minutes.

4. Stir in the flour and pour into a well-greased 2lb (900g) loaf pan.

6. Bake for 1 hour.

5. Remove from tin and cool.

6. Slice and spread with butter if desired.

Nutritional values

Calories: 102 kcal | Proteins: 1 g | Fats: 0.8 g | Carbs: 34 g

5.25 Fruit loaf

Prep time: 35 mins

Cook time: 1 hour 15 mins

Servings: 10

Ingredients

- Dried apricots 150g

- Figs 150g dried

- Pitted dates 150g

- Raisins 150g

- Orange juice 2 cups

- Bicarbonate of soda 1 tsp

- Brown sugar 3/4 cup

- Lightly beaten, 2 eggs

- Self-raising flour 2 cups

- Ground cinnamon 1 1/2 tsp

- Ground ginger 1 tsp

- To serve, butter

Instructions

1. Preheat your Oven to 180 C. Prepare a 7cm wide, 10cm x 21cm (bottom) loaf pan.

2. In a small saucepan, combine dried fruit & juice. Cook for 20 minutes, stirring until liquid is absorbed. Bicarbonate of soda Wait for 10 minutes.

3. Put the fruit mixture in a bowl. Add sugar and eggs. Add flour and spices. Gently combine. Pour into the loaf pan. A skewer placed into the center comes out clean after 50-55 minutes.

4. Baked for 10 minutes in the pan. Cool on a wire rack. Serve warm or toasted with butter.

Nutritional values

Calories: 239 kcal | Proteins: 2.9 g | Fats: 0.8 g | Carbs: 28 g

5.26 My Mother-in-Law's Plum Bread

Prep time: 15 mins

Cook time: 45 mins

Servings: 8

Ingredients

- Pitted 1 cup, chopped plums

- All-purpose flour 1 tablespoon

- Margarine ½ cup

- White sugar 1 cup

- Vanilla extract ½ teaspoon

- Eggs 2

- All-purpose flour 1 ½ cups

- Salt ½ teaspoon

- Baking soda ¼ teaspoon

- Plain yogurt ⅓ cup

- Brown sugar ¼ cup

Instructions

1. Preheat an oven to 350°F (175 degrees C). Spray or cover a 9x5-inch loaf pan using cooking spray.

2. Toss chopped plums using 1 tablespoon flour in a bowl. Set it aside. Beat the white sugar, margarine, and vanilla extract until smooth and creamy. Add the eggs, salt, 1 1/2 cup flour, and baking soda. Stir in the dry ingredients, alternating with the yogurt, until a smooth batter forms. Pour the mixture into the preheated loaf pan. Brown sugar on top of the batter

3. Bake for 45–50 minutes, or until a toothpick placed into the middle of the loaf falls out clean. Remove from oven and cool in pan for 10–15 minutes before slicing.

Nutritional values

Calories: 338 kcal | Proteins: 4.9 g | Fats: 12.9 g | Carbs: 51.4 g

Chapter 6: Cheese Bread Recipes

6.1 Bread Machine Cheese Bread

Prep time: 5 mins

Cook time: 3 hours 25 mins

Servings: 4

Ingredients

- Warm water 1 ½ cups

- Olive oil 4 tbsp

- Salt 1 ½ tsp

- White sugar 2 tbsp

- Shredded cheese 1 ½ cups (mozzarella, cheddar, parmesan, asiago, or your preferred cheese)

- Minced garlic 2 cloves

- Bread flour 4 cups

- Yeast 2 ¼ tsp

Instructions

1. Toss all the ingredients into the bread machine pan in the order listed, reserving 1/3 ounces of cheese for the top. If you don't have a Cuisinart bread machine, consult the proper order to add ingredients. If your manual specifies a different order, follow it.

2. Select "basic/white bread" as the bread type. Select the 2-pound loaf size and crust color of your choice. Select the dough setting if baking inside the oven. Allow the machine to complete the cycle by pressing the start button.

3. Baking in the Oven: Withdraw the kneading paddle at the end of the last kneading cycle. This is an optional step that can be completed after the bread has cooled. Brush the top and sides of the bread with an egg wash & top with the leftover cheese when it has finished rising. Remove the pan from the oven as soon as the bake cycle has finished.

4. To bake in the oven, remove the dough from the bread pan, punch it down, wrap it with a towel, and let it rise for thirty minutes in a warm area. Make a circle and oval out of the bread. Brush the top and edges of the pan with an egg wash, then sprinkle the remaining cheese on top. Preheat oven to 350°F and bake for 30-35 minutes. If the bread is done, it will sound hollow whenever tapped.

5. Before slicing, cool for 15-30 minutes on a wire rack.

Nutritional values

Calories: 290 kcal | Proteins: 11 g | Fats: 10 g | Carbs: 38 g

6.2 Bread machine cheese bread

Prep time: 30 mins

Cook time: 3 hours

Servings: 3

Ingredients

- Warm water 1 cup

- Unsalted butter 1/2 cup, melted

- Granulated sugar 2 teaspoons

- Kosher salt 1 1/2 teaspoons

- Shredded cheese 2 cups

- Bread flour 3 cups

- Rapid rise yeast 1 1/2 teaspoons

Instructions

1. Warm water, sugar, melted butter, and kosher salt go into the bread machine's pan. Sprinkle the shredded

cheese over the water mixture.

2. On the topping of the cheese, sprinkle the flour.

3. Sprinkle the yeast over the flour layer, ensuring there are no water spots.

4. Set your bread machine at BASIC; Moderate CRUST; 2LB loaf and put the baking pan inside.

5. Remove the pan from the bread machine whenever the bread is done and cool the loaf on a wire mesh rack.

6. Let the bread cool for at least ten minutes before cutting or storing, or until room temperature.

Nutritional values

Calories: 123.5 kcal | Proteins: 3.7 g | Fats: 2.6 g | Carbs: 21 g

6.3 Cheddar Cheese Bread

Prep time: 5 mins

Cook time: 1 hour 55 mins

Servings: 1

Ingredients

- Water 3/4 cup, room temperature

- Egg 1 large

- Salt 1 tsp

- Bread flour 3 cups

- Shredded cheddar cheese 1 cup

- Dry milk 2 tbsp, non-fat

- Sugar 2 tbsp

- Bread machine yeast 1 tsp

Instructions

1. Put the ingredients in the bread machine saucepan inside the sequence specified by the manufacturer, starting with the cheese and ending with the flour.

2. Basic/white bread cycle is recommended, with a medium/normal crust color option. Use the delayed-bake feature sparingly.

3. Changing the Dough's Consistency: After a few minutes of mixing, the ingredients should form a smooth ball all around the kneading blade. If the dough is too firm or soft, add a teaspoon of liquid or flour at a time until the desired consistency is achieved. No more than three to four teaspoons of liquid and flour should be added.

Because the machine cannot adapt to considerable fluctuations, the bigger volume of dough may not be baked thoroughly.

Nutritional values

Calories: 154 kcal | Proteins: 4 g | Fats: 2.9 g | Carbs: 34 g

6.4 Savory Cheddar Cheese Bread

Prep time: 5 mins

Cook time: 1 hour 10 mins

Servings: 1

Ingredients

- Milk 1 cup (227g), lukewarm
- All-purpose flour 3 cups
- Salt 1 1/4 teaspoons, (8g)
- Granulated sugar 1 tablespoon
- Grated cheddar cheese 1 cup
- Cheddar cheese powder ¼ cup
- Instant yeast 1 ½ tsp
- Tabasco sauce ½-1 teaspoon, optional

Instructions

1. Weigh your flour, or measure it in a cup by carefully spooning it in and wiping away any excess. Place all the ingredients in the bread machine's bucket in the sequence listed.

2. Set the machine to make basic bread with a light crust. Start by pressing the Start button.

3. After about ten minutes of kneading, check the dough; it created a cohesive ball that is slightly sticky. If required, add more milk or flour to achieve the desired consistency.

4. Allow the device to run through its entire cycle. Take the bread from the machine and place it on a cooling rack to cool.

Nutritional values

Calories: 130 kcal | Proteins: 5 g | Fats: 3.5 g | Carbs: 19 g

6.5 Beer Cheese Bread

Prep time: 10 mins

Cook time: 2 hours 10 mins

Servings: 1

Ingredients

- 1 package (1/4-ounce) active dry yeast
- Bread flour 3 cups
- Sugar 1 tablespoon
- Salt 1 1/2 teaspoons
- Unsalted butter 1 tablespoon, room temperature
- Beer 10 ounces, room temperature
- American cheese 4 ounces, shredded or diced
- Monterey jack cheese 4 ounces, diced or shredded

Instructions

1. Heat the beer & American cheese together on the stovetop or in the microwave until barely warm. The cheese doesn't need to melt. To combine the ingredients, stir them together.

2. Fill your bread machine pan halfway with the ingredients. Allow it to cool to warm if it appears to be too hot.

3. Add the other ingredients, choose white bread or the basic setting, and start the machine.

Nutritional values

Calories: 256 kcal | Proteins: 10 g | Fats: 8 g | Carbs: 33 g

6.6 Bread Machine Jalapeno Cheese Bread

Prep time: 5 mins

Cook time: 25 mins

Servings: 2

Ingredients

- All-purpose flour or bread flour, 3 cups

- Active dry yeast 1 1/2 teaspoons

- Warm water 1 cup

- Sugar 2 tablespoons

- Salt 1 teaspoon

- Cheddar cheese 1/2 cup, shredded

- Jalapeno peppers 1/4 cup

Instructions

1. In your bread machine, combine all ingredients in the sequence advised by the manufacturer.

2. If your bread machine has a dough function, use it (It usually runs around 90 minutes). After about 5 minutes, check the dough & add water and flour, a tbsp at a time, if it appears too dry or wet.

3. After the bread machine has finished, place the dough on a floured cutting board and knead it a few times before placing it in a greased 9x5 or 8x4 loaf pan. Allow approximately an hour of rising time after covering with a towel.

4. Bake for 25 minutes at 400 degrees or until it is firm and hollow when tapped. Allow cooling completely before slicing.

Nutritional values

Calories: 138 kcal | Proteins: 4 g | Fats: 2 g | Carbs: 24 g

6.7 Italian Cheese Bread

Prep time: 10 mins

Cook time: 2 hours 5 mins

Servings: 12

Ingredient

- Warm water 1 ¼ cups

- Bread flour 3 cups

- Pepper jack cheese ½ cup, shredded

- Italian seasoning 2 teaspoons

- Black pepper 1 teaspoon

- Parmesan cheese 2 tablespoons

- Brown sugar 2 tablespoons

- Salt 1 ½ teaspoons

- Active dry yeast 2 teaspoons

Instructions

Place the bread machine pan ingredients in the manufacturer's recommended order.

Choose between the White Bread or the Basic cycle. Start it.

Nutritional values

Calories: 37 kcal | Proteins: 1.8 g | Fats: 2.1 g | Carbs: 3 g

6.8 Cheese Buns Recipe

Prep time: 45 mins

Cook time: 2 hours 15 mins

Servings: 16

Ingredients

- Milk (divided), 1 cup (227 gr)

- All-purpose flour 3 cups, (divided), 360 gr

- Large 1 egg, 50 gr

- Heavy cream 1 tablespoon

- Yolk 1 egg, 14 gr

- Sugar 2 tablespoons (granulated), 24 gr

- Salt 1 ¼ teaspoon, 7 gr

- Softened butter 4 tablespoons, 113 gr

- Instant yeast 2 teaspoons, 6 gr

- Cheddar cheese 2 cups, 226 gr

Instructions

1. Making the dough: Tip: Before you start, measure out the whole amount of milk & flour you'll need (as specified in step #1).

2. Pour 1 cup of milk into a measuring cup. 3 cups flour, measured in a small separate bowl

3. In a large microwave-safe bowl, combine three tablespoons of the flour that just weighed out now and half of the milk (1/2 cup) to make flour paste. Cook for 1 minute on Maximum in the microwave, turning every 30 seconds. Cook for another 15-30 seconds if necessary, till the milk-flour mix is as dense as pudding.

4. Whisk the leftover 1/2 cup milk vigorously into the heated milk/flour mixture. It's fine if there are a few lumps left. They'll vanish during the mixing process. Place the dough in the bread machine pan.

5. Choose the DOUGH cycle and add the egg, heavy cream and egg yolk, salt, sugar, softened butter, leftover flour (save about 1/4 cup), plus yeast to the pan. "Start" should be pressed.

6. Check the dough after about ten min by opening the bread machine cover. If the dough is too wet, add a tablespoon of flour at a time until it is no longer wet. If the mixture is too dry, add a spoonful of milk at a time.

7. When the DOUGH cycle is completed, examine whether the dough has doubled in size. If this is the case, place it on a floured surface. If not, leave the dough in the machine till it has doubled in size.

8. Making the Rolls and Baking Them:

9. Place the dough on a floured surface after removing it from the bread maker. We prefer using a silicone mat since it is easier to clean (dishwasher).

10. The dough should be divided in half. Make a tidy ball out of each half, flouring the pan as you go to keep it from sticking.

11. Roll each dough ball into the13 x 9-inch rectangular with a rolling pin.

12. 1 cup of cheese should be evenly distributed across the top of a rectangle.

13. Divide the dough into four equal-sized strips longways, then half each strip short ways. There should be a total of 8 strips. Begin rolling each strip from one of the small ends.

14. Place the rolls in a spoke pattern in an 8 or 9-inch oiled (for optimum results, spray with Baker's Joy) pan.

15. Steps 2–6 should be repeated with the second half of the dough.

16. Cover pans with a tea towel or a cheap showering cap and let rise till nearly doubled. This will most likely take an hour, give or take an hour, depending on the room's temperature.

17. Once you believe the rolls are about ready to bake, preheat the oven to 375 degrees F.

18. Place the rolls on the oven's center shelf. Preheat oven to 350°F and bake for 14-17 minutes or golden brown.

19. Allow cooling for 5 minutes after removing from the oven. Slide a small knife around it to dislodge any cheese attached to the edge. Place the rolls on a cooling rack to cool for another 10-15 minutes. Using melted butter, coat the entire surface.

20. Tip: If you leave baked rolls in the pan for too long, they will sweat by becoming soggy just on the bottom.

Nutritional values

Calories: 194 kcal | Proteins: 7 g | Fats: 9 g | Carbs: 21 g

6.9 Cheese Bread Recipe for the Bread Machine

Prep time: 25 mins

Cook time: 1 hour 15 mins

Servings: 12

Ingredients

- Milk 3/4 cups

- Water 1/2 cups

- Beaten 1 egg

- Bread Flour 4 cups

- Shredded cheddar cheese 1 2/3 cups

- Sugar 3 Tablespoons

- Salt 1 teaspoons

- Active dry yeast 1 1/4 teaspoons

Instructions

1. Please keep in mind that this recipe is for a 2-pound bread machine. Make use of the default settings.

2. Regarding which ingredients to place in the bread machine first, follow the directions that came along with your bread maker. Just start with the liquid in the machine.

3. After 5 or 10 minutes of kneading, check on the dough. It ought to be a spherical and smooth ball.

Nutritional values

Calories: 244 kcal | Proteins: 10 g | Fats: 7 g | Carbs: 35 g

6.10 Garlic Cheese Italian Herb Bread

Prep time: 10 mins

Cook time: 4 hours

Servings: 12

Ingredients

- Milk, 1 cup

- Honey, 1 tbsp

- Butter ¼ cup, melted

- All-purpose flour, 2 2/3 cups

- Basil 1 tsp

- Oregano 1 tsp

- Italian seasoning 1 tsp

- Salt 1 tsp

- Active dry yeast 1 tsp

- Cheddar cheese ½ cup

- Asiago cheese ½ cup

- Minced garlic 5 cloves

- Butter 1 slice

Instructions

1. Toss all of the wet ingredients into the bread maker. Toss in the flour.

2. Toss the remaining dry ingredients into the bread maker's sides. Place yeast in the bread maker's center (absent from the salt). Place one butter strip on every edge of the bread maker. Begin with a full cycle.

3. Add shredded and cubed cheeses and garlic when the bread maker beeps for nuts and berries.

Nutritional values

Calories: 173 kcal | Proteins: 6 g | Fats: 9 g | Carbs: 36 g

6.11 Pepperoni Cheese Bread

Prep time: 10 mins

Cook time: 4 hours

Servings: 6

Ingredients

- Water 1 cup

- Butter 1 tablespoon

- Sugar 2 tablespoons

- Ground mustard 2 teaspoons

- Salt 1/2 teaspoon

- Cayenne pepper 1/2 teaspoon

- Garlic powder 1/4 teaspoon

- Active dry yeast 2-1/4 teaspoons

- Mexican cheese blend 1-1/2 cups, shredded

- Pepperoni 1 cup, chopped

- Bread flour 3 cups

Instructions

1. Put the first 9 ingredients in the bread machine pan in the sequence recommended by the manufacturer. Choose the most basic bread setting. If available, select a crust color & loaf size. Follow the bread machine's instructions for baking (examine dough after 5 mins of adding; add 1 to 2 tbsp. water and flour if required).

2. Add the cheese plus pepperoni a little before the last kneading (the machine may audibly suggest this).

1. Option to freeze: Wrap the cooled loaf with foil and freeze it in a freezer bag. Thaw over room temperature before using.

Nutritional values

Calories: 186 kcal | Proteins: 3.9 g | Fats: 6.6 g | Carbs: 29g

6.12 Cheesy Garlic bread

Prep time: 5 mins

Cook time: 2 hours

Servings: 2

Ingredients

- All-purpose flour 2 cups

- Baking powder 4 teaspoons

- Sugar 1 tablespoon

- Garlic powder 2 teaspoons

- Parsley flakes 1 teaspoon, dried

- Salt ½ teaspoon

- Milk 1 cup

- Egg 1, beaten

- Olive oil 2 tablespoons

- Italian blend cheese 1 ½ cups, shredded

Instructions

2. Combine the parsley flakes, flour, sugar, baking powder, garlic powder, and salt in the bread machine's pan.

3. Make a well in the middle of the dry ingredients and pour in the egg, milk, and olive oil.

4. Turn the bread machine into quick bread mode and let it preheat or knead the dough for you.

5. Whenever the bread machine asks you to add leftover ingredients, add the grated cheese. Close the top and let the machine finish baking the quick bread.

6. Remove the pan from the machine when the bread is done cooking and set it aside to cool.

7. When the bread is cold enough to handle, remove it from the pan and place it on a rack cooling rack to cool to room temperature before slicing & serving.

Nutritional values

Calories: 320 kcal | Proteins: 12 g | Fats: 7 g | Carbs: 38 g

6.13 Cottage Cheese Bread

Prep time: 15 mins

Cook time: 2 hours 5 mins

Servings: 12

Ingredients

- Loaf 2 lbs.

- Water 1/3 cup

- Cottage cheese 1 cup

- Egg 1 large

- Sugar 1 tbsp.

- Baking soda ¼ tsp

- Salt 1 tsp

- Yeast 2 tsp

- Bread flour 3 cups

Instructions

1. In the order specified, place the ingredients in the pan. The machine is set to light, but you can use any setting you choose.

Nutritional values

Calories: 154.6 kcal | Proteins: 6.1 g | Fats: 2.8 g | Carbs: 25.5 g

6.14 Cheese 'n onion bread

Prep time: 5 mins

Cook time: 3 hours 5 mins

Servings: 1

Ingredients

- Large loaf 3 cups

- Water **1 1/4 cups**

- Canola oil or Vegetable oil **1 tbsp**

- Hot pepper sauce **1 tsp**

- **White flour 2 cups**

- **Wheat flour 1 cup**

- Salt **1 1/2 tsp**

- Sugar **1 tbsp**

- Onion flake **2 tbsp, dried**

- Dried basil leaf **1 1/4 tsp**

- Cheddar cheese, **1/2 cup,** Cubed

- Bread machine yeast **1 tsp**

Instructions

1. Choose a loaf size.

2. Fill the machine with the ingredients according to the manufacturer's instructions.

3. Select the White Cycle option.

Nutritional values

Calories: 168.5 kcal | Proteins: 5.8 g | Fats: 4.7 g | Carbs: 28.6 g

6.15 Jalapeno Cheese Bread

Prep time: 10 mins

Cook time: 1 hour 25 mins

Servings: 4

Ingredients

- Water 1 cup, warm

- Yeast 2 ¼ teaspoons

- Sugar 3 tablespoons

- Olive Oil 2 tablespoons

- Bread Flour 3.5 cups

- Milk Powder 2 tablespoons

- Cheddar Cheese 4 ounces, about 1 cup

- Jalapenos 2, seeded, stemmed, or finely chopped

- Salt 1 teaspoon

- Optional, Vegetable oil,

- Like Pam, Cooking Spray

Instructions

1. To proof, the yeast, whisk together the water, yeast, and sugar in a mixing bowl or glass cup until thoroughly combined. Set it aside

2. Check the yeast after 10-15 minutes to see if it has a good froth layer, which indicates that it is still alive. Check your yeast when there is no froth layer. You'll have to try again if it's expired.

3. In the bread machine, pour olive oil into the bread pan. In the bread machine, pour the yeast mixture into the bread pan. In a bread pan, combine flour and milk powder. Toss the shredded cheese into the bread pan, then toss the chopped jalapeno. Season the bread pan with salt.

4. Set the bread machine to bake a light or dark loaf, depending on your preference. Alternatively, switch to dough only if you desire a regular-size loaf.

5. If you're producing dough, remove the dough ball from the bread maker and set it in a loaf pan greased with cooking spray. Cover with a cloth and rise for 20-25 minutes before baking as directed below.

6. Preheat the oven to 375 degrees Fahrenheit. Preheat oven to 350°F and bake for 25-30 minutes, or until golden brown. When knocked on the top, it should sound hollow.

7. Spread using butter and season with salt if desired.

Nutritional values

Calories: 216 kcal | Proteins: 8 g | Fats: 7 g | Carbs: 31 g

6.16 Homemade cheese and pepperoni bread

Prep time: 10 mins

Cook time: 2 hours 25 mins

Servings: 1

Ingredients

- Garlic salt 1 ½ teaspoons
- Sugar 2 tbsp
- Mozzarella cheese 1/3 cup
- Warm water 1 cup
- Dried oregano 1 ½ tsp
- Bread flour 3 ¼ cup
- Active dry yeast 1 ½ tsp
- Pepperoni ⅔ cup, diced

Instructions

1. Put the very first seven ingredients in the bread machine pan in the sequence recommended by the manufacturer.

2. Choose the most basic bread setting.

3. Choose a crust with a medium hue.

4. Add the pepperoni just before the final kneading (the machine should beep at this point).

5. Make a 1 1/2 pound loaf of bread.

6. For this recipe, do not use the delay timer feature.

Nutritional values

Calories: 193 kcal | Proteins: 9 g | Fats: 12 g | Carbs: 51 g

6.17 Cheesy Garlic Pull-Apart Rolls

Prep time: 20 mins

Cook time: 3 hours 40 mins

Servings: 8

Ingredients

For the dough

- Bread Flour 420 grams (3 ½ cups)
- Organic cane sugar 2 tbsp
- Salt 1 tsp

- Oil 4 tbsp

- Instant Yeast 7 grams (2 ¼ tsp)

- Water 1 cup (85 deg F)

For the toppings

- Salted butter 4 tbsp (melted)

- Garlic 4 tbsp (finely chopped)

- Shredded cheese 1 cup (mozzarella)

- Rosemary 1 tsp

Instructions

1. In a bread machine, make dough.

2. Add the components (water, bread flour, sugar, salt, oil, yeast) in the order suggested by the manufacturer, depending on the type of bread Machine. "Dough" is the cycle to choose.

3. Mix the butter, garlic, and rosemary in a bowl while the dough prepares.

4. The dough will have gone through its first rise after the "Dough" cycle is completed.

5. Take the dough from the bread maker and place it on a flat surface.

6. The dough is shaped

7. For around 30 seconds, knead the dough on the lightly floured surface.

8. Make little balls out of the dough and lay them in a baking dish. As they will rise, keep them about 1 centimeter apart.

9. Using a basting brush, slather the balls in the butter garlic & rosemary mixture, making sure they are evenly coated.

10. Shredded cheese should be sprinkled just on balls and even in the spaces between them.

11. Ascend to the top

12. For around 90 minutes, cover the baking tray with a second tray. You may also leave the pan in the oven for 5 minutes on "Warm" mode and then let them rise in the oven for another 90 minutes.

13. Oven-baking

14. Preheat oven to 350° F once balls have risen.

15. Preheat the oven to 350° F and bake the rolls for 20 minutes.

16. Once the melted cheese and the rolls turn golden brown, the cheesy garlic pull-apart rolls are ready.

Nutritional values

Calories: 364 kcal | Proteins: 20 g | Fats: 17 g | Carbs: 43 g

6.18 Gluten-Free Cheddar Cheese Bread

Prep time: 10 mins

Cook time: 4 hours 10 mins

Servings: 14

Ingredients

Wet ingredients

- Eggs 3

- Water 1 ½ cups

- Vegetable oil 2 Tbsp.

Dry ingredients

- Active dry yeast 2 ¼ tsp.

- White rice flour 2 cups

- Rice flour 1 cup, brown

- Dry milk powder ¼ cup

- White sugar 2 Tbsp.

- Poppy seeds 1 Tbsp.

- Dill weed 1 ½, dried

- Xanthan gum 3 ½ tsp.

- Salt 1 tsp.

- Cheddar cheese 1 ½ cups, shredded

Instructions

1. Place all wet ingredients at room temperature in a medium mixing bowl and stir well.

2. Combine all of the dry ingredients in a large mixing bowl. To make sure everything is properly combined, use a wire whisk.

3. Add all wet ingredients first with your bread machine's pan, then the dry ingredients on over.

4. Choose setting 3 – entire wheat – and push the start button.

5. Keep a spatula handy for the first 5 minutes or so to press the mixture down and ensure it's thoroughly mixed.

6. Remove the gorgeous, long-awaited loaf from the pan and cool on a cooling rack after it has finished cooking for around 4 hours.

Nutritional values

Calories: 234 kcal | Proteins: 7 g | Fats: 8 g | Carbs: 32 g

6.19 Artisan Asiago Bread

Prep time: 25 mins

Cook time: 4 hours 15 mins

Servings: 24

Ingredients

- 3 bread flour (Gold Medal), ½-3 3/4 cups

- Sugar 1teaspoon

- Regular active dry yeast, 1package (2 1/4 teaspoons)

- Warm water 1 1/4cups (120°F-130°F)

- Vegetable oil or olive oil 2tablespoons

- Dried rosemary 2teaspoons if desired

- Salt 1teaspoon

- Diced Asiago 1 1/4cups, Swiss or any other solid cheese

Instructions

1. Combine sugar, 1 1/2 cups flour, and yeast in a large mixing bowl. Fill the bottle halfway with warm water. 1 minute on low speed with a whisk or an electric mixer, scraping bowl often. Wrap securely in plastic wrap and set aside for 1 hour, or until bubbling.

2. Combine the oil, rosemary, and salt in a mixing bowl. 1/2 cup at a time, stir in the remaining flour until a soft, homogeneous dough forms. Allow 15 minutes for cooling.

3. Place dough on a floured work surface. Knead the dough for 5 to 10 minutes, or until smooth and springy. 1 cup of the cheese should be kneaded in. Using shortening, grease a large mixing bowl. Place the dough in the bowl and turn it to butter on both sides. Cover bowl securely with plastic wrap and set aside for 45 to 60 minutes, or until the dough has gotten bigger in a warm area. If the indentation stays when the dough is touched, it is ready.

4. Using shortening or cooking spray, lightly butter an uninsulated cookie sheet. Place dough on a floured work surface. Stretch sides of dough downwards to produce a smooth top and shape into a football-shaped loaf, approximately 12 inches long. Place the loaf on a cookie sheet with the smooth side up. Using a floured pastry brush, generously coat the loaf. Cover loosely with plastic wrap and set aside for 45 to 60 minutes, or until the

dough has about doubled in size.

5. Place an 8- or 9-inch square pan just on the bottom rack of the oven and fill it halfway with hot water. Preheat the oven to 450 degrees Fahrenheit.

6. Using cool water, mist the loaf and then dust it with flour. Carefully cut a 1/2 inch-deep slash crosswise down the center of the loaf with a serrated knife. In the slash, sprinkle the remaining 1/4 cup of cheese.

7. 10 minutes in the oven Reduce the preheat oven to 400 degrees Fahrenheit. Bake for another 20 to 25 minutes, or until the bread is deep brown and hollow when tapped. Cool on a cooling rack after removing from the cookie sheet.

Nutritional values

Calories: 128 kcal | Proteins: 3.7 g | Fats: 2.8 g | Carbs: 32 g

6.20 Plaited cheese and herb bread

Prep time: 1 hour

Cook time: 25 mins

Servings: 1

Ingredients

For the bread

- 500g white bread flour, Allinson's Strong

- Salt 1 tsp

- Granulated sugar 1 tsp, Unrefined & golden

- Butter 15g (softened)

- Bake yeast, 7g Easy

- Warm water 325ml

- Mixed herbs (basil, chopped finely, oregano, parsley), 10g Dried

- Parmesan 25g

For the top

- Egg 1 (for the glaze)

- Cheddar cheese 10g (grated)

Instructions

1. To make the dough, gently mix all of the bread ingredients and gradually add the water till you reach the

appropriate texture (you may not need the full quantity).

2. Knead the dough for 5 minutes in a mixer with a dough hook attached or 10 minutes by hand. Knead for another 5 minutes if mixing by hand.

3. Divide the dough into three equal pieces, then roll into long, equal-length sausages.

4. To keep the dough strands in place, braid them together, tucking the ends somewhere under the dough.

5. Brush the dough with the egg and place it on an oil baking tray. Cover with a lightly oiled plastic wrap and rise until doubled in size.

6. Preheat oven to 190°C and set the timer for 20 minutes.

7. Grated cheddar cheese should be sprinkled over the top of the loaf. Preheat oven to 350°F and bake for 35 minutes or golden brown.

Nutritional values

Calories: 148 kcal | Proteins: 7.6 g | Fats: 9.4 g | Carbs: 36 g

6.21 Oregano and Romano Cheese Bread

Prep time: 10 mins

Cook time: 2 hours

Servings: 16

Ingredients

- Bread flour 3 cups
- Water 1 cup
- Freshly grated cheese 1/2 cup (parmesan or romano)
- Sugar 3 tablespoons
- Leaf oregano 1 tablespoon, dried
- Olive oil 1 1/2 tablespoons
- Salt 1 teaspoon
- Active dry yeast 2 teaspoons

Instructions

1. Follow the manufacturer's instructions when adding the ingredients to the bread maker.

2. Set the level to basic or medium, then press the start button. Enjoy the wonderful scent.

3. A 1 1/2-pound loaf of bread is made from this recipe.

Formless Oven-Baked Loaf

1. Use the dough cycle in the bread machine to make the bread.

2. Take the dough out of the machine and roll it into a round loaf.

3. Cover the loaf with a wet kitchen towel and place it on a wax paper-lined baking sheet.

4. Allow it to rise for 40 to 50 minutes, or until it has doubled in size.

5. Preheat the oven to 400 degrees F and bake for 20 - 25 minutes or golden brown.

Nutritional values

Calories: 61 kcal | Proteins: 2 g | Fats: 3 g | Carbs: 7 g

6.22 Filipino Cheese Bread

Prep Time: 30 mins

Cook Time: 15 mins

Servings: 4

Ingredients

Dough

- High-grade flour 3 1/2 cups

- Potato flakes 1/2 cup

- Active dry yeast 1 tbsp

- Warm water 1/4 cup

- Butter melted 1/2 cup

- Milk 1 cup

- Sugar 3/4 cup + 1 tbsp sugar

- Salt 1/2 tsp

- Egg 1

Cheese Coating

- Grated cheddar cheese 2 cups

- Powdered milk 1 cup

- All-purpose flour 1/2 cup

- Powdered sugar 1 1/4 cups

- Butter, 1/4 cup cut into small cubes

Instructions

1. Combine active dry yeast, warm water, and sugar in a mixing bowl. Place it in a warm place for 10 minutes before serving.

2. Whisk the butter, milk, sugar, and salt in a mixing bowl until thoroughly blended.

3. In a separate bowl, combine the yeast and water.

4. Gradually add the flour & potato flakes, then switch to the kneading hook and knead for ten min if using a tabletop mixer. If not, lay the ingredients on a floured area and knead it by hand for ten minutes once it is shaped into a ball.

5. Place the dough in a greased or nonstick bowl, cover with a wet towel, and let it rise for an hour or until it has doubled in size.

6. Prepare your cheese coating by combining all cheese coating ingredients in a large blending bowl and mixing with a spatula till it resembles rough crumbs. Remove it from the equation.

7. Take the dough and divide it into three equal halves. Roll each part into a long log, then cut into 7-10 pieces (7 if you want a bigger cheese bread, 10 if you want a smaller cheese bread), roll each piece into a small bowl, then roll it in the cheese coating mixture, carefully pushing the mixture into the dough. The cheese coating should be thoroughly applied.

8. Place the prepared piece in a baking pan coated with baking paper, then repeat with the remaining dough.

9. Place the baking pans with the bread in a warm area for 30 minutes or until it has risen to 1 1/2 of its original size (do not over-rise).

10. Preheat the oven to 150°C and bake for 15 minutes, or until golden brown.

Nutritional values

Calories: 150 kcal | Proteins: 2 g | Fats: 9 g | Carbs: 16 g

6.23 Garlic, Herb & Cheese Bread Rolls

Prep Time: 25 mins

Cook Time: 20 mins

Servings: 4

Ingredients

For rolls

- Warm milk 1 cup (100 – 110°F)

- Olive oil 1 tablespoon

- Eggs 2 whole

- Granulated sugar 2 tablespoons

- Fine salt 1 1/2 teaspoons

- Garlic powder 1 teaspoon

- Garlic 2 cloves, *minced*

- Minced fresh rosemary 1 tablespoon

- Minced fresh thyme 1 tablespoon

- Instant yeast 2 1/4 teaspoons (1 packet)

- All-purpose flour 4 cups

For topping

- Egg 1 large

- Grated Parmesan cheese 1/3 cup

Instructions

1. In the bowl of a stand mixer, combine the milk, salt, garlic powder, oil, eggs, sugar, garlic, rosemary, thyme, and yeast. 2 cups flour, stirred in with a wooden spoon till the dough forms a shaggy, rough lump

2. Attach the dough hook to the mixer, reduce the speed to medium-low, and slowly add the remaining flour, kneading till a dough mass forms. Only add as much flour as the dough requires to come together. Knead for another 4 to 5 minutes on medium-high speed, or until a soft, smooth ball of dough forms. To the touch, the dough should be elastic and slightly tacky. Only add more flour if the dough is too sticky to handle.

3. Place the dough in a big clean bowl that has been lightly sprayed with cooking spray. Wrap plastic wrap around the dish gently. Allow the dough to rise for 1 hour at room temperature or until it is puffy and nearly doubled in size.

4. Using cooking spray, coat a 13x9-inch baking pan. Deflate the dough gently. Divide the dough into 15 equal pieces using a bench scraper, spatula, or pizza wheel.

5. Place each piece in the prepared pan and roll it into a tight ball. Cover the dough lightly with plastic wrap and then let it rise for 1 hour, or until it has about doubled in size.

6. Preheat oven to 375 degrees Fahrenheit.

7. Whisk the egg in a small bowl, then carefully brush it over the rising rolls. Parmesan cheese should be uniformly distributed on the buns.

8. Preheat the oven to 350°F and bake the rolls for twenty minutes, or till golden brown. Warm leftovers may be stored in a plastic bag for up to 3 days.

Nutritional values

Calories: 282 kcal | Proteins: 12 g | Fats: 14 g | Carbs: 25 g

6.24 Irish Cheddar Soda Bread

Prep Time: 10 mins

Cook Time: 40 mins

Servings: 12

Ingredients

- All-purpose flour, 2-1/2 cups

- Baking powder 2 teaspoons

- Baking soda 1 teaspoon

- Salt 1 teaspoon

- Cold unsalted butter, 4 tablespoons cut into 1/2-inch chunks

- Extra sharp 8 ounces cheddar cheese

- Low-fat buttermilk 1-1/4 cups

- Egg 1 large

Instructions

1. Preheat oven to 375 degrees Fahrenheit. Using butter and nonstick cooking spray, grease an 8-inch round cake pan.

2. Combine the flour, baking soda, salt & baking powder in a large blending bowl

3. Add the chilled butter and toss to combine. "cut" the butter into the flour mixture using the pastry cutter or two butter knives until the mixture is crumbly, with some pea-size chunks of butter remaining. Add the shredded cheese and stir to combine.

4. Mix the buttermilk as well as the egg in a separate bowl. Stir in the wet ingredients until everything is well moistened. Do not overmix the ingredients.

5. Place the sticky dough in the pan that has been prepared. Using floured hands, push the dough against the pan's edges. Bake for 40-45 minutes, or till golden brown and a cake tester inserted in the center comes out clean. Allow 5 minutes for the bread to cool in the pan before turning it out onto a cooling rack. Serve heated with softened butter and cut into wedges.

6. Freezer-friendly, the bread may be frozen for up to three months if needed. Wrap it tightly in plastic wrap and set it in the freezer after totally cooling. To reheat the bread, cover it in aluminum foil and place it in a 350°f oven when it is warm.

Nutritional values

Calories: 221 kcal | Proteins: 9 g | Fats: 11 g | Carbs: 22 g

6.25 Brazilian Cheese Bread

Prep Time: 10 mins

Cook Time: 20 mins

Servings: 6

Ingredients

- Olive oil or butter ½ cup

- Water 1/3 cup

- Soy milk or milk 1/3 cup

- Salt 1 tsp

- Tapioca flour 2 cups

- Minced Garlic 2 tsp

- Grated parmesan cheese 2/3 cup

- Eggs 2 beaten

Instructions

1. Preheat the oven to 375 degrees Fahrenheit (190 degrees C).

2. In a large saucepan, combine the olive oil, milk, water, milk, & salt and heat on high. Remove from heat as soon as the mixture reaches a boil and toss in the tapioca flour and garlic till smooth. Allow ten to fifteen minutes for resting.

3. Mix the cheese and egg into tapioca mixture until blended; the mixture should resemble cottage cheese in texture. Drop the mixture into rounded, 1/4 cup-sized balls onto an oiled baking sheet.

4. 15 to 20 minutes in a preheated oven until gently browned the tops.

Nutritional values

Calories: 385 kcal | Proteins: 6.3 g | Fats: 22.6 g | Carbs: 39.9 g

6.26 Cheesy Bread

Prep Time: 15 mins

Cook Time: 5 mins

Servings: 20

Ingredients

- Shredded mozzarella cheese 4 ounces (1 cup)

- Shredded sharp 8 ounces (about 2 cups) cheddar cheese

- Chopped green onion 1/4 to 1/2 cup (to taste)

- Mayonnaise 1/4 cup

- Sour cream, 1 tablespoon optional

- Garlic, minced 1 to 2 cloves

- Unsalted butter, 1/2 stick (1/4 cup, 2 ounces)

- French or Italian bread 1 loaf

Instructions

1. To make the cheesy topping, whisk the butter and garlic in a small bowl until creamy. Combine the cheeses and green onion in a separate large mixing dish. Combine the mayonnaise & sour cream in a mixing bowl. Combine the butter and cheese in a mixing bowl.

2. Spread cheese on the bread as follows:

3. Preheat the oven to broil. Lay the crust side down on a foil-lined baking sheet after slicing the loaf in half horizontally. Cover the bread with the cheese mixture.

4. Put under the broiler for 3 to 5 minutes, or until beautifully browned.

5. Remove the slices from the broiler and set aside for 5 minutes until they are cool enough to handle. Using a bread knife, cut the bread into slices. Serve.

Nutritional values

Calories: 199 kcal | Proteins: 6 g | Fats: 14 g | Carbs: 12 g

---

6.27 Cheese Garlic Bread

Prep Time: 10 mins

Cook Time: 15 mins

Servings: 1

Ingredients

- Multi-grain bread 1 and 3/4 slices

- Garlic 1

- Black pepper as required

- Butter 2/3 tablespoon

- Mozzarella 2 and 3/4 tablespoon

- Salt as required

For Seasoning

- Oregano as required

- Chili flakes as required

Instructions

1. First, to make wonderful cheese garlic bread, bring the butter to room temperature in a mixing bowl. To make the garlic butter, combine it with the smashed garlic. Take the multi-grain bread pieces and spread them with butter. Preheat the oven at 200 degrees Celsius in the meanwhile.

2. Sprinkle a handful of shredded mozzarella cheese on top of each one. Make sure the cheese is fully set and not slipping off the bread pieces. Season oregano, chile flakes, black pepper, and salt to taste each piece of bread.

3. Place the slices on a baking sheet and bake in the preheated oven. Bake for 8 to 10 minutes at the same temperature, or until the cheese has melted and become golden brown. It's time to eat your handmade cheese garlic bread. Serve immediately with a spicy dip.

Nutritional values

Calories: 199 kcal | Proteins: 6 g | Fats: 14 g | Carbs: 12 g

6.28 Georgian Cheese Bread

Prep Time: 20 mins

Cook Time: 15 mins

Servings: 12

Ingredients

For Dough

- Warm water 1 cup (200 milliliters)
- Instant yeast 1 tablespoon
- All-purpose flour 2.5 pounds (1.15 kilograms)
- Warm milk 1 cup (200 milliliters)
- Olive oil 1.7 ounces (50 milliliters)
- Egg 1 large
- Sugar 1 teaspoon
- Fine salt 1 teaspoon
- Additional warm water 1 cup (200 milliliters) as needed

For Cheese Filling

- Sulguni cheese, grated 7 ounces (200 grams)
- Eggs are divided 3 large
- Butter, optional 1 tablespoon (20 grams)

Instructions

To Make Dough

1. Collect the necessary ingredients.

2. Combine warm water and yeast in a small bowl and leave aside.

3. Combine flour, milk, oil, sugar, salt, egg, and yeast-water mixture in a large blending bowl or stand mixer. Knead the dough by hand or by a dough hook until smooth and elastic. (Up to 1 cup more warm water may be required.)

4. Cover bowl with oiled plastic wrap and set aside to rise for 2 hours in a warm location.

5. Divide the dough into three pieces after punching it down. Before shaping, cover with oiled plastic wrap and set aside for 15 minutes.

To Make Cheese Filling

1. Collect the necessary components.

2. Combine shredded cheese, 1 egg, plus butter, if using, in a medium mixing bowl. One egg should be separated, with the yolk kept and the white saved for later purposes. Set aside the egg yolk after blending it with a fork.

To Assemble Acharuli Khachapuri

1. Preheat the oven to 400 degrees Fahrenheit. Each dough ball should be rolled into a boat shape.

2. Fill each of the three dough boats with equal amounts of cheese filling. As seen in the photo, fold the sides and ends of the dough.

3. Bake khachapuri for 12 minutes on a parchment-lined cookie sheet (to collect any melted butter or cheese).

4. Remove the khachapuri from the oven and brush the dough (not the cheese) with the remaining beaten egg yolk. In the middle of the cheese, crack the final egg.

5. Return to the oven for 3 minutes, or until the yolk is still runny and the white hasn't set completely. With a huge pat of butter, serve right away.

Nutritional values

Calories: 556 kcal | Proteins: 28 g | Fats: 33 g | Carbs: 37 g

6.29 Garlic Cheese Bread

Prep Time: 15 mins

Cook Time: 10 mins

Servings: 4

Ingredients

- Grated cheddar 3 ½ cup

- Grated pepper jack ¾ cup

- Grated parmesan ½ cup

- Mayonnaise ½ cup

- Softened butter 1 ¼ sticks

- Whole green onions 4

- Salt 1 dash

- Fresh ground pepper

- Garlic 4 cloves

- French bread 1 load crusty

- Flat-leaf parsley ½ cup chopped

Instructions

1. Preheat oven to 375 degrees Fahrenheit.

2. Combine the cheeses, mayonnaise, 1/4 stick melted butter, and green onions in a mixing bowl. Season with salt to taste, then put aside or store in the refrigerator until needed.

3. In a skillet over medium-low heat, melt the remaining 1 stick butter and add the garlic. Cook for a few minutes to let the garlic flavor come through.

4. Make a half-loaf of bread. Brush each half with the garlic butter, ensuring it's equally spread. Spread the cheese mixture over the loaves and bake for 10 minutes, or until the cheese is hot and bubbling.

5. Sprinkle the chopped parsley on top after the dish has come out of the oven. Cut into slices and serve.

Nutritional values

Calories: 130 kcal | Proteins: 5 g | Fats: 7 g | Carbs: 13 g

6.30 Italian Cheese Bread

Prep Time: 5 mins

Cook Time: 13 mins

Servings: 4

Ingredients

- Refrigerated pizza dough 1 (13.8-oz) tube

- Italian dressing 3 to 4 tbsp

- Grated parmesan cheese 2 tbsp

- Garlic powder ¼ tsp

- Dried oregano ¼ tsp

- Dried thyme ¼ tsp

- Shredded mozzarella cheese 1 cup

Instructions

1. Preheat the oven to 400 degrees Fahrenheit. Using parchment paper, line a baking sheet.

2. Roll out the pizza dough on parchment paper after unrolling it.

3. Spread Italian dressing on top of the pizza crust. Over the dough, sprinkle parmesan cheese, oregano, garlic powder, and thyme. Shredded mozzarella cheese is sprinkled on top.

4. Bake for 13 to 15 minutes, or until cheese is melted and crust is golden brown.

Nutritional values

Calories: 130 kcal | Proteins: 6 g | Fats: 6 g | Carbs: 12 g

6.31 Bacon and Cheese Bread

Prep Time: 10 mins

Cook Time: 50 mins

Servings: 4-6

Ingredients

- Self-rising Flour 1 1/4 cup

- Salt 1/2 tsp

- Sugar 3 tbsp

- Back Bacon, 200 g fried and roughly chopped (7 oz)

- Cheddar cheese, grated 1 cup

- Parsley, chopped 2 tbsp

- Vegetable Oil 2 tbsp

- Eggs 2 extra-large

- Milk 3/4 cup

Instructions

1. Preheat the oven at 180 degrees Celsius (350 degrees Fahrenheit) – Cooking spray a cake pan and loaf pan and lay the bottom with baking paper

2. Sift together the flour, salt, and sugar – Stir in the bacon, cheddar, and parsley until everything is well combined.

3. Whisk together the oil, eggs, and milk; add to the flour mixture and stir thoroughly.

4. Bake for 50–60 minutes, and when a tester comes out clean, after transferring the mixture to the prepared pan.

5. Remove from oven and cool for 5 minutes in the pan before turning out onto a cooling rack.

6. Warm or at room temperature is OK.

Nutritional values

Calories: 160 kcal | Proteins: 8 g | Fats: 6 g | Carbs: 17 g

Conclusion

Do you have a hunger pang? It could be difficult to read so much about bread manufacturers. Read our Ultimate Bread Machine Cookbook Guide if you're ready to take your bread machine to the next level.

Bread is a baked dish that may be made using a variety of doughs. Typically, flour and water are used to make the dough. Hundreds of different forms, sizes, flavors, and textures of bread are produced. The proportions and kinds of flour and other components used and the techniques used to prepare them to differ. Bread has been one of the most fundamental meals throughout history and one of the earliest artificial foods. People have been baking bread since the beginning of agriculture.

Bread is served differently from any meal of the day in all civilizations. It may be consumed as part of a meal or as a standalone snack.

A bread machine, frequently known as a bread maker, is kitchen equipment used to bake bread. The gadget comprises a bread pan and tin with built-in paddles in the middle of a tiny multi-purpose oven. Bread machines may make various bread, including whole wheat bread, gluten-free bread, rye bread, and hundreds of others. This book involves several recipes for fruit and cheese bread specifically.

Made in the USA
Coppell, TX
14 April 2022

76599582R00066